Domestic Violence in OUR Church?

Written by Johnnie Lorren

Edited by Charles Mills

Come and Reason Ministries believes that God is love and all life is built to operate in unity and harmony with our Creator. However, a destructive principle has infected and altered God's design for life and is the root to pain, suffering and ultimately death. We believe that eternal healing is experienced when we are reconciled into unity of love with God, possible through the achievements of Jesus Christ, which leads to an intelligent cooperation with God in practicing His methods and principles in our daily lives. Therefore, Come and Reason Ministries has developed these study guides to refocus our minds upon God - His character of love and His design for life, health and eternal happiness. It is our hope that in utilizing these guides you will experience not only greater intimacy with God, but actual transformation of being such that God's methods of Truth, Love and Freedom will become your methods, actually applied and lived out today. So, come and reason through the abundant evidence God has provided of his unending love, supreme trustworthiness and life enhancing nature of his methods.

Author: Johnnie Lorren
Editor: Charles Mills
Layout and Cover Design: Tamara Slocum
Published by: Lennox Publishing

Come and Reason Ministries
P.O. Box 1344 Collegedale, TN 37315
www.comeandreason.com

ISBN-13:978-0-9858502-1-0

CONTENTS

INTRODUCTION..1

WEEK 1: God's Design for Intimate Relationships...........................3

WEEK 2: Satan's Plan to Destroy the Home.................................17

WEEK 3: Women's Roles in Home, Church, and Society............................31

WEEK 4: Types of Abuse...44

WEEK 5: Man's Far-Reaching Role as Husband and Father.......................55

WEEK 6: Passing It Down...67

WEEK 7: The Bible's Standard for Relationships............................81

WEEK 8: How Children Learn to Be Abusers.................................95

WEEK 9: Does God Abuse His Power?.......................................109

WEEK 10: Detecting Need Within a Church Family...................123

WEEK 11: Tools of the Trade...137

WEEK 12: My Role...151

WEEK 13: Hope for the Future..163

Domestic Violence in OUR Church?

Introduction

We've all seen them - the startling programs on TV highlighting stories of families torn apart by abuse. Perhaps we even know someone in our own neighborhood or family who has experienced domestic violence. Yet, it's easy to believe that Christian homes are different—that "we" are different. Surely when people become church members, that type of abuse stops!

Think again. Recent research indicates that the percentages of domestic violence among Christian intimate partners are as high and, in some categories, even a bit higher than in non-Christian homes. We will review those numbers later. But for now, just take a moment to soak in that reality—and a moment more to ask "Why?" That's exactly what we'll be doing in the next 13 weeks as we review not only case histories (names have been changed), but also reasons for abuse and its effect upon partners (victim and abuser) and children. We will also discover how abuse affects the church as a whole, and we will pursue Biblical counsel.

God is no respecter of persons. Neither is abuse. The Father of Lies has seen to that. Yes, we'd love to be able to say that once a person publically commits to Christianity, those tendencies fade into nonexistence. That, however, is not the case. We will also see that although the major portion of abuse is husband to wife, it can happen in reverse. And, the numbers show unequivocally that being in a position of leadership may raise the level of the temptation to control and abuse rather than diminish it.

Did you see that seven letter word CONTROL? Remember that word. And don't be surprised if you catch little reflections of yourself as we reflect on the reality of humanity and our need for control. Our goal is 1) to see where an unhealthy desire to control comes from, and 2) from whom it does not come. In doing so, we will clarify the often misused label: "Act of God."

Remember this: Although our Heavenly Father is the most powerful Being, the Creator, our Savior, and although He has all strength and could wipe us out in an instant, He never uses His sovereignty in an unhealthy manner. Read that twice if need be because from this premise—this truth—we will identify the true source of this destructive behavior.

God is love. He doesn't just love—He is love. He doesn't just forgive—He is forgiveness. His character is so completely love, He can do no other. Despite how God gets the blame (those "Acts of God"), we can find another source for inappropriate power use. Love cannot be forced. If you've never thought about God in this light, it may sound a bit radical. You may be inclined to skip over this subject or discount it completely. Your discomfort level may be rather high. But don't ignore it. You may discover the real reason for abuse and how you can help defuse it.

Is this new territory for churches? Yes. But it's absolutely imperative information. We've kept our heads in the sand long enough. Secrets have allowed dysfunction to ruin homes and lives long enough. We've caused sadness in the heart of our loving Heavenly Father long enough. What can we do? For starters, we can generate the courage to become informed from a proper paradigm. This information may change your life.

Domestic Violence in OUR Church?

WEEK 1

God's Design for Intimate Relationships

DAY 1   Heavenly Leadership

LIVING WORDS

"We know that 'all of us possess knowledge.' This 'knowledge' puffs up, but love builds up" (1 Corinthians 8:1).

"Love is patient and kind; love does not envy or boast; it is not arrogant or rude. It does not insist on its own way; it is not irritable or resentful" (1 Corinthians 13:4-5).

BOTTOM LINE

Being "like Him" is reflecting that kind of treatment toward others. Period.

SETTING THE STAGE

Why is it important to understand what God is like as leader of His family? Does misunderstanding God's approach change earthly families? Does family dysfunction explain church dysfunction? Dare we take a critical look into why we are losing most of our young people out the back door of our churches? Is there any hope?

In this first week we will discover how abuse in any form disconnects us from our source of life. God doesn't disconnect. We do. God uses every method available to remind us that the battle is not ours to win. We can only imagine that His heart of love is hopeful that He will at last find a people who "get it"—who are tired of trying to prove their way of thinking is the only right way (theologically, psychologically, politically), a people who will finally discover how to lovingly draw all men (and yes, families) to Him.

THINK ABOUT IT

Has your heart ever been melted by a strong-arm technique? Probably not. It is simply impossible to prove yourself right and be intimate at the same time. Want to change things? Read on.

DAY 2   Daring to Address Issues

LIVING WORDS

"'For the man who does not love his wife..., says the Lord, the God of Israel, covers his garment with violence" (Malachi 2:16).

"Wives, submit to your own husbands, as to the Lord....
Husbands, love your wives, as Christ loved the church and gave himself up for her" (Ephesians 5: 22, 25).

BOTTOM LINE

God never condones abuse. Period. So, how do abusers rearrange this Biblical counsel?

SETTING THE STAGE

We've taken the first steps into this controversial, hidden, not-for-the-faint-of-heart subject. No one wants to believe the church is ignoring such a huge issue. Is there anything we can do about it anyway? Will bringing domestic violence out of the closet cause separation in our church? Will it compromise our safety? Wouldn't it be better to just "let it lie"? Let's look at an actual interview with Gloria, someone who understands the topic first hand. (Names have been changed.)

"I've got a five month old...and I was pregnant. Well, Jason packed up and left....[He] was so mad I was pregnant again...[as if] I did it all by myself! I almost lost [one] baby from him hitting me in the stomach before he left. I called the cops, and Jason threatened me. I couldn't answer the door. You try to put it behind you and let it go cause this was a daily thing... some days weren't as severe as others. He wouldn't quit hitting me and I was just on the floor begging him to quit and [2-year-old] Todd was screaming 'quit hitting my mommy.' I was screaming and he was grabbing my hair and kicking me all the way down the hallway to our bedroom."

Gloria and Jason were both church members as are all the people mentioned in the stories highlighted here. Many hold offices in their home churches. Some are leaders. This lady had grown up in an abusive home, and was drawn to just such a relationship in marriage. She escaped with her life, which is more than some are able to do. Satan was successful in destroying this home and greatly damaging the lives of both partners and the children.

We spend millions on evangelism. We feel exhilarated when we increase numbers on the church pews. Yet within our own walls there are innumerable hurting souls, too afraid to speak up, too exhausted to ask for help. "It's none of my business," we say. "She's just a bit crazy, that's all. He would never do that." And on it goes.

THINK ABOUT IT

1) If this were my daughter, what would I do? 2) What will happen to the children? 3) Has she been to see the pastor and was it effective? 4) What are the resources for this mother/wife? 5) Are there *any* reasons this abuse is deserved? 6) Is God allowing this to "teach her a lesson"?

NOTES

DAY 3   Submit vs. Control

When the Lord said, "I will put enmity between you and the woman" (Genesis 3:15), He was not talking to Adam! God's design for creating man and woman and uniting them in marriage was so that we could understand the relationship God wants to have with us.

His favorite metaphor centers on the bride. When the bride and groom become one and are truly united (not engulfed, not void of healthy self), the beauty that results is not only creative, but fulfilling and healing. It seems that unity in diversity is absolutely possible. Think how different we are from God, yet He desires oneness—atonement, "at-one-ment"—with us. So it should be in the earthly home. How else will we represent the true character of God to the world?

QUESTION

What does the Bible mean by "submit?" The Apostle Paul writes: "Wives, submit to your own husbands, as to the Lord" (Ephesians 5:22). Is it supposed to be only one way in a relationship? Do we believe that God requires us to submit to Him blindly or arbitrarily? Could this belief affect our homes?

Perhaps you've grown up being taught to "submit" to the Lord unquestioningly. "God says it, I believe it, and that's good enough for me!"

CONSIDER THIS

As a child, we are told by parents what to do. Hopefully, in their wisdom, they will gently begin letting us make decisions that are age appropriate. When we are 30, we don't routinely go to our parents and say "Tell me what to do!" A more mature suggestion might be "Please give me some advice." So it should be with God. Asking Him to make us a puppet and direct every step of our day (What shall I wear? Should I turn left or right? Do I deserve to be treated well?) demonstrates immaturity. It doesn't mean God leaves us. But how wonderful it would be if, gradually, our character would become enough like His so that, as a friend, we could converse, reason, and grow within the circle of life He has designed. If He created us for His pleasure, it seems reasonable to assume He would want us to be a pleasurable friend!

In such a dynamic, growing relationship, would any show of force, control, or abuse be appropriate? When someone says "No" and another person tries to *force* him or her to change that response, that's abuse. The abuse may be emotional, physical, sexual, financial, health-related, or even religious. All are tremendously damaging.

THINK ABOUT IT

Are there scenarios you can play out in your mind concerning your own home that fit into the "abuse" category? We are not talking about occasional missteps. We all fall short of what we wish we were. But are there patterns—continual incidents that involve control of any kind? Those are the ones we need to identify and address. How can we help others if we do not remove the beam in our own eye?

NOTES

DAY 4   Looking at Functionality

QUESTION

What does a "functional family" look like? There are myriads of books on dysfunction in men, women, children, families, even organizations, ad nausea. We may need a refreshing look at what is functional. Let's try.

TAKE A LOOK

Recently at a preschool graduation, a father shared celebratory cake with his four-year-old son who had been in blue cap and gown only minutes before. When the little fellow used one arm of his new white shirt for a napkin, Dad requested nicely that he not do that, then quickly reassured him with a smile, saying, "It's OK, son." There was no condemnation. No hint that the child had disappointed. No "you don't measure up" message. That is good family function.

When a husband praises his wife for something she has done well in front of his or her friends (whether she is present or not), that is good family function. Other examples include: forgiveness given quickly after working through differences in a relationship, asking if there are household chores where one spouse can assist another, thinking ahead in plans for togetherness, and including each other in those plans, spending quality time with each child, continuing the courtship atmosphere into marriage, being a good provider not a workaholic, expressing empathy during physical illnesses, protecting family without being overprotective, lifting one another up rather than making the other feel "less than," having one healthy goal financially, surprising others in word or action that lets them know you've been thinking of them, creating an atmosphere of security and acceptance, companionship that includes freedom to choose,

> **" WHEN A HUSBAND PRAISES HIS WIFE FOR SOMETHING SHE HAS DONE WELL IN FRONT OF HIS OR HER FRIENDS (WHETHER SHE IS PRESENT OR NOT), THAT IS GOOD FAMILY FUNCTION. "**

and realizing that "submitting" works both ways and includes every part of the relationship. That's functional.

Functionality rubs off on children. Isn't that nice! It also rubs off on everyone around you - at work, in church, and in every life operation. So does dysfunction ("to the third and fourth generation"—Numbers 14:18), unfortunately. So why would the hater of men's souls spend so much time trying to ruin the family?

If he can get us to believe that God is a liar and "in it for Himself," then Satan has us. He's fine with us wanting to "be like God" as long as our picture of God is skewed.

Nothing is more important than understanding who God is and how He has designed His universe to run. There is no more imminent need than for Christians to see the truth about God. That's why Satan is out to destroy the very vestige of God's character. He has been at it since the war in heaven.

NOTES

DAY 5 Why God Desires Family Unity

QUESTION

Why does God desire that His children enjoy united, loving, forgiving family units?

Everyone is part of a family somehow, even if they are not married. God has wonderful designs for single Christians just as He has for families. There are always ways we can show others caring and love that expresses the best of our Heavenly Father. No individuals are to be left out in this eternal plan, no matter their status on earth. Christ died for *all*. Of course, not all will accept that free gift of His sacrifice, and sadly—after many attempts at reconciliation—God will have to let them go.

Why does He do that? Because He is mad at them, hates them, is good and ready to wipe them out? Have you ever applied to God the Father an attribute that you yourself would never use on your earthly child (or even a friend)?

One preacher, in describing the closing events when Christ comes down to earth and His enemies are ready to storm the city and destroy it, said of God: "It's party time! There will be great rejoicing at the death of His enemies." The man backed it up his conclusion with statements and texts. The nagging question that speaker needed to consider is: "You mean to tell me that if your son was outside those gates, you'd be inside dancing and partying?"

Sometimes, we transform God into the worst of evil-hearted murderers with a word, a phrase, a concept perhaps learned from youth. "He will get even. He will take revenge. He will show His power. God means to be obeyed no matter what! His laws are arbitrary, and we better obey or else. He sends terrible troubles to teach us a lesson! Don't mess with God. Never argue with Him. Never question. God rewards the good and destroys the wicked. God chooses whom He wants to save and whom He wants to destroy and they have no choice. Furthermore, He has created a lake of fire that burns forever to torture those he has chosen to torture."

Perhaps it would be well for each of us to spend a thoughtful day writing down what we believe and what those beliefs say about God.

1 John 4:18 suggests that "there is no fear in love, but perfect love casts out fear. For fear has to do with punishment." Notice how much fear exists in the paragraphs above that portray God as angry and vengeful.

So, who really is the author of fear, of death, of destruction, and of lies? These are the tools of the evil one. He can't use truth as a tool because he is not truth. But he certainly knows how to take truth and twist it, change it, convincing us that God is not safe to trust. We must ask: Who is God, really?

THINK ABOUT IT

Ask yourself: What were you *told* God is like? Write that down. Then write about this: Having experienced God in your life, what do you now believe Him to be? Is there a difference? Is God your friend?

NOTES

DAY 6 Our Need to Know God

BOTTOM LINE

Love can't be forced.

"I wouldn't have to do this to you if I didn't love you so much." That statement often used by abusers is a good example of how truth and scripture can be twisted. To know what love really is, we must look at Jesus. His example never shows Him misusing His power. In fact, He laid it aside to become one of us.

He loved everyone. He drew everyone—especially children—to Him. It's said that children and animals can sense a good heart, and these little ones knew! They felt it in His touch, His smile, His acceptance.

Mary Magdalene found it in His forgiveness, the blind man, His touch. The widow saw His strength and love as her son was restored to her. Should they have chosen to see, even the Pharisees could have witnessed His tears as He reminded them of their deviousness.

Somehow, in their human state, even His disciples had difficulty seeing the true God in their master. Is it any wonder we find it difficult at times? Yet, our loving Heavenly Father never gives up, never quits giving us all the evidence we need, never locks us out from His Spirit until and unless we finally choose not to believe the truth so completely that He will sadly let us go.

So, why can't I just take everything on blind faith? Isn't it good to just believe? Isn't that sufficient?

We're told that Satan believes and trembles (James 2:19). Of course he knows who God is, what God is really like. But to win his war against all that's good and truthful, Satan lies. Most cunning of all, he can make a lie sound just like a truth. Knowing this, is it then safe to "just believe" everything that sounds spiritual or religious? If it is promoted by a church, by our church, can we safely believe without question?

Everyone worships something, or someone. We were designed to worship. Many say we have a "God-shaped" void in our hearts that only He can fill. Perhaps many dysfunctional relationships form from trying to fill that void inappropriately. The deceiver of people is always ready to insert into a life someone or something that will distort God's love.

Which begs the question: Is it even possible to know God? With permission, here is a section of a Christian woman's journal that addresses that very issue: "I wonder, is it really possible? How dare I, this small, tired, often discouraged creature with thin hair, baggy eyelids, and aching body—how dare I hope, believe, assume, that I could have the right to talk with, walk with, and have a friendship with the God of the universe? Talk about arrogance! Or perhaps it's simply naiveté—the sanguine in me. Well, something in my woman's (little girl's) heart longs for just such a relationship." That longing is evidence of that God-shaped void.

THINK ABOUT IT

What does knowing God look like—what would change about me that others could see? What if there really isn't a God or heaven? Is my longing to get to heaven a selfish motive?

NOTES

DAY 7 Resources and Direction

DON'T STOP NOW!

You can expedite your learning process by spending some valuable time in these resources:

sdaabuseresponse.org (Southern Adventist University's committee on domestic violence—website)

thehotline.org (National Domestic Violence Hotline)

theraveproject.org (excellent training and information from a Christian perspective)

Battered to Blessed: My Personal Journey by Brenda Walsh, Pacific Press Publishing, 2005

Domestic Violence: What Every Pastor Needs to Know by Rev. Al Miles, Fortress Press, 2011

Violence in Families: What Every Christian Needs to Know by Rev. Al Miles, Augsburg Books, 2002

Servants or Friends? Another Look at God by Graham Maxwell, Pineknoll Publications, 1992

Toward a Growing Marriage by Gary Chapman, Moody Press, 1985

An Endless Falling in Love by Ty Gibson, Pacific Press Publishing, 2003

And of course, *The Bible*. Pick up a new one and try this: Go through the New Testament first, and at the end of each book, write: "What does this tell me about God?"—then list those things. You may be surprised!

TALK ABOUT IT

This has been a heavy week. Don't despair. There are resources. There's hope. We as a Christian community can become the lighthouse for those who are hurting. We can study to know the true God, not one that has been portrayed from childhood by well-meaning parents or teachers as someone to be feared. We can become comfortable asking questions, revisiting doctrines, rethinking decisions. Because we have a choice, and because beliefs change us, what we believe is so very important. Therefore, we will want to continually ask God to give us the Spirit of Truth and a longing for it.

A huge part of the hope for abused individuals includes training through Christian organizations, sermons addressing the issues openly, advocates being appointed in churches, and victims being helped. This is an exciting time, and we can be a part of it.

If truly understanding God's character can change how we as Christians treat people, we can see how becoming informed, empathetic, and willing to help can make a huge difference in our Christian community. Learning to be loving and lovable Christians is still the best sermon, bar none.

The goal of this 13 weeks is to know God as He *truly* is, and to find ways to share that *really* good news with those struggling with abuse.

AND FINALLY...

What we will be discovering in the weeks ahead could make you more of an "informed prisoner," or a wonderfully informed first responder. It's your choice. Knowing what to do in time of crisis is very rewarding. Let's learn how to put shoes on the gospel commission!

Domestic Violence in OUR Church?

WEEK 2

Satan's Plan to Destroy the Home

DAY 1 Devious Leadership

LIVING WORDS

"Jesus said, 'Daughters of Jerusalem, do not weep for me, but weep for yourselves and for your children' " (Luke 23:28).

BOTTOM LINE

Destroy the family, and you've destroyed one of God's greatest mirrors of Himself.

SETTING THE STAGE

Christ, already having been through tremendous abuse, spoke to women who would be marginalized. No one was better equipped than Jesus to know what was going to happen to these dear souls.

If you were the destroyer of nations, how would you go about accomplishing complete destruction? You could attack those nations with overt operations. You could cut off supplies of food, or destroy theirs. Yes, you could fly airplanes into their treasured structures to incite panic. But wouldn't it be much more effective to create distrust within the individual members of those societies, to find ways to cause civil wars, to pit neighbor against neighbor and brother against brother? If you could instill enough fear within those territories, you might just be able to sit back and watch the destruction without doing much else. But, where would you start?

It is said that the hand that rocks the cradle rules the world. (Early videos of Stalin, Castro, and Hitler would be interesting!) While we can't blame every defect of character upon parents, wouldn't the home be the obvious choice of a terrorist who wished to destroy a nation? Those who were willing to die—who flew the airplanes into the New York skyline—believed that God was directing them. Who rocked the cradle of their belief?

THINK ABOUT IT

Is it possible to be sincere, and be sincerely *wrong*? Absolutely!

DAY 2   Where It All Began

Let's go back to those war days in heaven. "Now war arose in heaven, Michael and his angels fighting against the dragon. And the dragon and his angels fought back" (Revelation 12:7).

Who was Satan before he chose to turn against God? His name was Lucifer, which means Light Bearer. He was in a position of great leadership. But it wasn't enough. Jealousy caused him to turn against Christ. His problem wasn't with God. It was with God's Son. He knew exactly where to aim his attack.

Although Satan and his angels were cast from heaven to this earth, he continues to try to prove himself right, by twisting Christ's own words to fit his lies.

Interestingly, word-twisting is an abusive technique. It can make victims feel inferior and confused, even doubting their own identity. Christ did not doubt His identity, but humanity is programmed through sin to do just that. An abuser knows how to do it effectively. "You never do anything right." "Why can't you see that if you'd change, everything would be OK?" "You're supposed to do exactly as I say and not question!"

> **"ABUSIVE WORDS ARE LIKE A KNIFE, CUTTING AWAY AT ONE'S SOUL UNTIL COMPLETE CONTROL IS IN PLACE."**

Even the proverbial rolling of the eyes as a public response to something a spouse says can generate deep feelings of inferiority. Given enough attack time, victims can totally lose their ability to feel viable, even though they may be qualified professionally or in other ways.

Abusive words are like a knife, cutting away at one's soul until complete control is in place. The abuser is an artist at this "surgery." Unless there is intervention, the patient can die on the operating table, either emotionally, or physically.

Victims—usually women—may have come from a home where one parent was abusive, and learned to "submit" no matter what. They may have heard their own mother say "If I continue to be a good Christian wife, sooner or later your daddy may change."

Their "normal" is abnormal and dysfunctional. But, they know no other way.

Along comes an admirer/suitor looking for someone to control. He knows all the right words to say and soon they are united for life. The honeymoon period is rapidly over and she learns too late that she has fallen from the frying pan into the fire. Mother says she must stick it out ("You made your bed; you must lie in it!") no matter what. God requires it. And the saga continues.

NOTES

DAY 3   Disbelief Concerning Domestic Violence

"Churches will do much to protect the unborn from the hands of an abortionist but little to protect the unborn from batterers." (*No Place for Abuse*, Kroeger & Nason-Clark, p. 83).

Interview most victims of domestic abuse and they will tell you that church members will surround families of cancer victims yet allow those on the receiving end of abuse to suffer silently and without support. They will tell you that the "holy hush" within Christian organizations is what has caused many victims to delay or refuse sharing what is happening in their homes, because people don't believe them. They hear us sing hymns like "Happy the Home," yet allow doctrinal interpretations to proliferate painful existences in those families who buy into the perceived right of controlling others.

While there are a few well-known televangelists whose lives have been publicized, for the most part, spiritual leaders are shielded. Many abusers are simply moved from one location within an organization to another, their habits hidden a bit longer. Where are the leaders who will call to account those men or women who will ultimately lose their connection to God if they don't change their ways? We do a disservice to the abused and abuser when we hide the problem.

There's even more to the problem than we realize. *God's* honor is at stake! We carry His name as Christians. No wonder those outside of church organizations look on and say "I want no part in it, if *that's* spirituality." Christ says, "I, when I am lifted up from the earth, will *draw* all people to myself'" (John 12:32, emphasis added). The messages we are actually sending out must not be expressing Christ's drawing power or there might be one hundred converts where there is now one.

HAVE YOU?

You may have heard statements like these: "If it was really happening in our church, we would have heard more about it." "Maybe across the ocean, but not in my congregation!" "I know that man. He would never even say a bad word, let alone hurt his wife." "What did *she* do to cause him to have to do that?" "Why doesn't she just leave if that is really happening?" "There's nothing I can do. Talking about it just makes it worse." "No one will want me to be in leadership next year if I bring *that* up!" "I have enough problems of my own. I don't want to know about the problems of others."

One of the authors quoted above, Pastor Catherine Clark Kroeger, herself a childhood victim of abuse, wonders aloud about why she stayed in the church and why she even became a minister. She thought it might represent sanctuary to her. At five years old, she didn't have many choices. But as she grew, she began to see that the church seemed to actually support abuse—certainly not in an overt way, but possibly by way of omission. She feels that everything has to do with the interpretation of Bible texts. Interesting.

NOTES

DAY 4   Why Our Children Run

QUESTION

What's wrong with using power and control?

There are whole conventions and training programs designed to teach you how to control your present life, your staff, your finances, and your future. We believe that influencing others is not only effective, but our right. Indeed, influence plays a part in everyone's life. It's a God-given tool. Used appropriately, it encourages growth and healing while beautifully representing God. In the hands of the Father of Lies, it can turn deadly.

Watch two or three siblings—ages two and up—play together for any extended time, and you'll soon discover what humankind has known for centuries. Humans are all about self-preservation. Me first. Me *only*! We come by it naturally. Of course that "naturally" now carries the label of sin. Self-centeredness holds no small power over us. Maturity—especially spiritual maturity—comes slowly it seems, and *rarely* in many instances.

Because of this, we tend to picture God in a powerful, controlling role—fiery scepter in hand, warning us not to misstep or we will die. Incorrectly, we hear that message through religious voices, as proof that God is "watching us from a distance," "making a list and checking it twice," and that perfection is His expectation...or else. This sounds, not surprisingly, like the underlying proclamations found within abusive homes!

But there's a problem with this type of environment. The more we feel "watched" the more we fail. Condemnation breeds failure. Where's the hope, the joy, the beauty of God? No wonder our youth flee out the back door as soon as they are on their own. Now they have choices whereas before, they didn't. We really can't blame them. Do you want to spend eternity with a God who arbitrarily makes up rules, punishes you if you fail to keep every last one perfectly, and perhaps decides ahead of time who will live, who will die, or who will burn eternally? You'd be heading for the back door of that relationship, too!

THINK ABOUT IT

You are leading a youth group of fifteen individuals with varying backgrounds. As you talk with them week after week, you've discovered much disbelief, fear, and misunderstanding. Some have openly expressed cynicism. Others sit with folded arms and express few if any words. But you see there are questions.

1) How would you go about showing them who God really is, and that Christ and God are the same in spirit and purpose? How would you put human shoes on the divine gospel?

2) A member of this group comes to you in private and shares a bit about the abuse going on at home toward his/her mother and younger sister. How do you handle this information? How do you maintain loyalty to this young person while providing help?

3) Can you remember something you were taught as a young person that now sounds absolutely ludicrous to you in reference to your Heavenly Father? What changed your mind?

NOTES

DAY 5 Pastoral Guidance

In defense of leaders and pastors, there are many who are willing to counsel, protect, and work with victims of abuse. This is becoming more of a reality every day as information and training become increasingly widespread and accessible. The last thing we want to do is throw the baby out with the bathwater, believing that *all* leaders are misusing their influence and power. This is simply not true.

When a pastor maintains a deep love for his Lord, and when he is open to continual learning despite the possibility of poor earlier training, that pastor has chosen to walk the walk, not just talk the talk. He/she can be of invaluable help. The pastor may, indeed, be the first point of contact.

In a study of women of faith who experienced domestic violence, many interviewed victims longed for a pastor they could turn to who would believe them. That was, in fact, one of the greatest needs among women interviewed. They needed to know someone would believe them. Given the hidden nature of most abuse, that is understandable.

Knowledgeable pastors will know when to counsel, and when to refer to professionals. But they will never suggest couple's counseling. Why? Because the abuser will always overshadow the victim and the victim will likely shut down. That scenario will not change, except that there may be heavier abuse as a punishment to the victim for speaking up. Therefore, couple's counseling is never recommended in domestic violence cases.

The safety of the victim—and children—should always be considered. Is it safe to go home? Is there a safe place to stay? A large percentage of deaths happen when a victim tries to leave and the abuser feels he/she is losing control. Doesn't this seem similar to the attacks of the devil when he thinks he's losing us? What a tangled web he weaves!

QUESTION

Does the victim stay and take it in order to stay alive? Will that help? There are no easy answers.

"Just pray more, dear," or "You should just be a better wife and this won't happen," is not good counsel. Remember this: *nothing* a wife has done makes it OK to abuse. Every story has two sides. But no matter how codependent or untrained a wife or husband may be, there is never an excuse for abuse.

So, is it OK for God to abuse, just not us? How dare we say that God would abuse His children! How could a God who *is* love even think of doing such a thing?

THINK ABOUT IT

Why does God allow abuse? Does He want to punish the abuser, or would He prefer to heal him/her? What does He mean by "forgiving seventy-seven times" (see Matthew 18:22)? Does forgiving someone mean we must trust the person again?

NOTES

DAY 6   Tangled Webs

QUESTION

If Satan is trying to tear apart Christian homes, shouldn't we do everything in our power to stay together no matter what is happening behind closed doors?

Carol Cannon, in her book entitled *Hooked on Unhappiness*, says it this way: "Research suggests that the children of divorced parents and the children of parents who remain unhappily glued together have the same kinds of self-esteem problems in later life. Why? The children of couples who stay together in spite of their misery are caught in the crossfire. I've yet to meet the first adult or child reared in this kind of hostile environment who appreciated their parents' noble sacrifice" (p. 75).

She goes on to explain that children will blame themselves for the parents' unhappiness and that, oftentimes, parents use the kids as an excuse to punish each other. This counselor of many isn't making a case for divorce. She says she is making a case for growing up and getting healthy, for recovering no matter what it takes.

Carol further states, "Consider this: the minute I start trying to control your behavior, I'm operating on the premise that I know what's best for you or that I have a corner on knowledge of God's will" (p. 95).

Shaming someone for saying "no" isn't OK. Manipulators may make sideways hints instead of direct requests, passive-aggressively controlling while feeling good about *not* being a controller. Carol says "Some perfectionists, especially those who practice their perfectionism in the context of religion, need to start by assessing their theology and developing a more accurate understanding of God's character. Hopefully they will discover that God's love and approval don't fluctuate on the basis of their performance" (p. 94).

One woman in the process of recovery requested that God place a "big screen TV" in her path, showing her what she was really like. "He did," she said, "and it was painful." But her immense relief during the learning experience has made it all worth it. The surprise was that she was abusing herself! Now there's a habit very hard to break.

But it is possible. Make a list of how many times a day you say "(Your name), you crazy idiot - why did you do *that*?" Then learn to replace such negative statements with warm, loving ones like "OK, that wasn't the best solution. But I can do this...." Self-abuse isn't any more comfortable than having someone else aim it at you.

THINK ABOUT IT

When someone tries to tromp on my boundaries, how do I treat them? Is that abuse? If I don't *have* boundaries, am I abusing myself by letting people walk on me? Is allowing someone else to interpret God's will for me like allowing them to play God? Is taking charge of myself healthy? Self-control is one of the spiritual gifts listed in the Bible. What would be an unhealthy way of controlling myself?

NOTES

DAY 7   God's Techniques

DON'T STOP NOW!

When fear takes over, it does us well to remember who in this battle for eternity is the stronger. Stronger in what? Everything.

God's strength lies so beautifully in His character framed by life-giving freedom. God does not use the tools of deceit and lies to get "one up" on His adversary. Because we have been given the ending to the story—as recorded in Revelation—we know the "good guys" win—not by might, not by power, but by love.

TALK ABOUT IT

"I am the Alpha and the Omega" (Revelation 1:8). The proclamation "I AM WHO I AM" is comforting to some but fear producing to others.

Some have put the Bible aside because of the "scary" stories. Others bathe daily in the incredible waters of His word. Why the difference?

While in nature, we watch the cocoon reveal the awesome butterfly and exclaim to a watching child, "This beauty is because God is love!" Then we see the hungry lion pouncing on his prey as one more of God's lovely creatures loses its life. How do we explain that?

God speaks through our daily lives. His guidance, comfort, and protection say a lot. "Humbug!" says the non-believer who has amassed millions. "*I* did this, not God!" Nearby, a street lady in rags is convinced that God has forgotten her. She is dying, with no hope for the future. How do you address the millionaire, and the dying indigent?

From some ornate pulpit on Broad Street a preacher assures his flock that God is with them day and night; that "everything" comes from God—both good *and* evil events, and we should accept it from His hand as His sovereign will. Just down the street, kneeling beside his bed, a young man prays in vain for God to heal his mother. Where is God in the good times, and in the bad?

AND FINALLY...

In his book *Dangerous Wonder*, Michael Yaconelli writes: "What would happen if we all took Jesus' advice and became 'like little children'?...Why, then, don't more of us experience life this way? Because we allow obstacles to squelch our wonder and steal our souls." Don't stop asking questions! It's OK with God" (p. 23)!

NOTES

Domestic Violence in OUR Church?

WEEK 3

Women's Roles in Home, Church, and Society

DAY 1   Freedom?

LIVING WORDS

"The women should keep silence in the churches. For they are not permitted to speak, but should be in submission, as the Law also says" (1 Corinthians 14:34).

BOTTOM LINE

Was it law or custom that commanded women's silence in Paul's day?

SETTING THE STAGE

Many of us live in the good ol' USA where our freedoms were fought for and won. Granted, there are still countries where the social and/or religious structure does not allow full freedom, especially in the area of marriage. Atrocities toward women (and men) create horrendous living conditions. America has tried to intervene at times, but the job is overwhelming. The "End It Now" project which has garnered millions of signatures is one effort by the Christian community. There are others.

Without using force to make everyone believe the same as we, how do we make a difference? But, do our efforts arise from our belief that it is right and loving, or are we simply on a soap box? What are people who have the "mind of Christ" and the heart of our Heavenly Father supposed to do?

It's my prayer that there will be a natural outpouring of God's Spirit within our own ranks and in our communities. Such an outpouring can be a powerful catalyst for much-needed change.

DAY 2   Customs and Beliefs

It's relatively easy to compare the customs of free countries today with the customs in Jesus' time. Wouldn't it seem odd if women were totally silent in a modern house of worship? Who would sing? Who would lead the children? Who would give wise counsel to the younger women? How would the "housekeeping" items needed each week be coordinated? Could a delicious potluck be prepared without speech?

No, we don't spend much time trying to press today's women into the mold of Christ's time. Christ himself never put them in a box and shut the lid. Women played important roles in His ministry. He enjoyed inspiring conversations with them and He honored them openly. Christ's own mother spoke at a wedding feast, instructing workers to carefully follow Jesus' words. It's unimaginable that Christ would silence women at every turn. Not once did He place women in a bad light, belittle them, or embarrass them. What then should a loving husband do as he strives to be like Christ?

" IT'S UNIMAGINABLE THAT CHRIST WOULD SILENCE WOMEN AT EVERY TURN. NOT ONCE DID HE PLACE WOMEN IN A BAD LIGHT, BELITTLE THEM, OR EMBARRASS THEM."

Paul's command that women remain silent must have been in response to a particular problem faced by a particular church at that time. It obviously wasn't in response to a command from God. That's not to say that area customs aren't important. There are many churches today where women are not invited to speak because of cultural dictates. Out of respect for (but not necessarily in agreement with) that culture, women remain silent.

But, in any church that follows the model structured by God alone, women enjoy the freedom to speak their minds and share in the ongoing life of their spiritual community.

However, in some people's minds—and these people can include church leaders—God appears narrow-minded and looks at men and women differently. Such a position can create deep-seated hostility and division within the church.

THINK ABOUT IT

Is it possible that a husband's (or wife's) view of God and His character makes a huge difference in how they treat others? Could working from a legalistic, dogmatic paradigm—believing that God says "do as I say or I will have to kill you"—seeing God as vindictive, vengeful, and controlling, direct someone to "be like Him" and utilize those tactics on their loved ones or fellow church members? The answer is—yes!

NOTES

DAY 3   Domestic Violence Clarified

Domestic violence refers to a pattern of violent and coercive behavior exercised by one adult in an intimate relationship over another. Another way of putting it is that any act intended to instill fear and exert control over another person is abuse!

Family violence, as described by one church entity, is as follows: "Family violence involves an assault of any kind—verbal, physical, emotional, sexual, or active or passive neglect—that is committed by one person or persons against another within a family, whether they are married, related, living together or apart, or divorced" *(from the General Conference of Seventh-day Adventists' official statement, "Family Violence," adopted August 27, 1996).*

Let's take that definition into the practical zone and identify some abusive ways a spouse may be treated:

1. **Emotional Abuse:** Ignores your feelings; ridicules or insults you in a group about your beliefs, actions, looks, religion, etc.; withholds approval, affection, or appreciation as punishment; criticizes you continually; keeps you from having a job, controls your money, makes all the decisions; regularly threatens to leave; punishes or deprives the children when angry at you; threatens to kidnap or kill the children if you leave; tells you about his/her affairs; harasses you about affairs he/she imagines you are having.

2. **Physical Abuse**: Pushes or shoves you; slaps or bites you; kicks or chokes you; hits or punches you; throws things at you; locks you out of the house and puts you in danger; abandons you in dangerous places; refuses to help when you are sick, injured, or pregnant; subjects you to reckless driving to frighten or control you; threatens or actually hurts you with a weapon; forces you off the road or throws you out of a car.

3. **Sexual Abuse**: Treats you as a sex object and assumes you would have sex with others; insists you dress in a more sexual way; minimizes the importance of your feelings about sex; criticizes you sexually; withholds sex and affections; insists on

unwanted attentions; calls you bad sexual names; publically shows sexual interest in others; has affairs; forces sex with him/her or others; commits sadistic sexual acts.

The family violence document listed above includes these words: "The Bible clearly indicates that the distinguishing mark of Christian believers is the quality of their human relationships in the church and in the family. It is in the spirit of Christ to love and accept, to seek to affirm and build others up, rather than to abuse or tear one another down. There is no room among Christ's followers for tyrannical control and the abuse of power or authority."

I believe that the members of God's church on earth have a responsibility to care for those involved in family violence and to respond to their needs.

THINK ABOUT IT

List some ways that church members can be of help to victims of abuse using the Biblical principles of love and acceptance. How do you imagine Christ would treat victims of abuse?

NOTES

DAY 4   Are Church Leaders Immune?

Historically, women—more than men—have been the victims of abuse. However, abuse can be directed either way in a relationship. Perhaps that's inevitable in a world where sin reigns. Someone tends to lead, and someone tends to follow.

This damaging condition is no respecter of persons, and those in church authority can fall victim as well. The problem lies in two areas: 1) leadership techniques and 2) the reasons why a follower chooses to follow a leader. Let's examine both.

CONSIDER THIS

First, consider these questions: Are leaders always God ordained? Does personality play a part in how they lead? Can people be trained to be leaders? The answers, as I see it, are no, probably, and yes.

A study of brain quadrants and personality styles can usually identify a person as a leader or a follower, a giver or a taker, servant or friend. Watch any group of children playing and you'll pick out the leaders in five minutes flat. Watch a bit longer, and you can tell who will quietly do their own thing despite the leader, those who will follow wherever they are told, and those who want to be the leader but can't ease into that slot no matter how hard they try. The same applies at any grade of education, business environment, or in the home.

Leaders can be chosen, self-appointed, or voted in arbitrarily. And therein exists a real challenge. But, there's help when it comes to the Christian home.

God designed the man to be the leader of the home. Thankfully, He also provided some very specific instructions on *how* to lead. Those instructions can be distilled into one command: *Allow choices!* But to be effective, leadership must enjoy and *share* the benefits of choice. What's clearly missing from God's model for leadership are the elements of control and force. A leader is actually someone who *serves the needs* of followers! Christ's life is a perfect example of this seeming contradiction. Leaders, in the mind of God, also serve.

We're beginning to understand that abuse is built on the twin dangers of control and force. Societies today view leadership as a position of control. Our "dog-eat-dog" mentality strengthens this concept. Climb over, step on, scratch and claw, get to the top of the heap no matter what you have to do in the process! So much of life is built around that philosophy. Such thinking serves as the foundation of domestic violence and abuse. If you want to stop the abuse, you must change the philosophy that's being used as the cornerstone for that abuse.

THINK ABOUT IT

Christians believe they are different. And yes, we should be. Perhaps it would be wise for each of us to personally take a look at where we stand and ask, "Am I different from the world?" This is especially true if you're a leader in your church, in your family, in your circle of friends, community, or government. "How did I get there? Are there walking wounded along the side of the road that I traveled in order to get here? Or did I allow the grace and teachings of Christ to transform me into a true leader, full of serving and giving, teaching and promoting others, creating an environment of freedom?"

NOTES

DAY 5   Why She Stays

Centuries past have definitely laid down a pattern: Men lead, women follow. But such a custom within our own country (United States) has shifted for a number of reasons. The fall of the American family may have pushed the leadership skills of women to the forefront. They are, in huge numbers, now "head of the household." In fact, statistics from 2010 reveal that 41% of children in the U.S. are born to unwed mothers.

With that in mind, what keeps so many women who are victims of abuse from understanding that they have choices, that they can not only survive but thrive on their own? Why does a woman under attack withdraw tighter into her protective shell and not ask for help?

Often, it's because the abuser has convinced her she is not capable of living without him. She couldn't survive—she thinks—emotionally or financially. Besides, she made a promise "until death do us part," right? More than three thousand times a year, in the USA alone, death is exactly what happens—she dies at the hand of her husband.

So, why does she stay? The reasons are many: she believes she can't make it on her own, she still loves him and hopes he will change, she thinks the kids need both parents no matter what, she fears for her life or that of her children, he apologizes and promises to do better, there is no one she can talk to that she trusts, he keeps drawing her back with gifts before the abuse starts again, or she doesn't want to feel like she has failed.

If the "little girl" inside her has always felt like she didn't deserve much, it's very hard to find a reason to shake her fist and say "I won't be treated this way. I deserve better!" If that little girl inside thinks God ordained men to rule over women in whatever way they desire (perhaps as her own father did), it would be very difficult to believe that she has the right to be happy. And, if she has lost trust in mankind, it's hard to reach out to anyone who might help.

Why does she stay? Because she believes she has no other choice. But she's wrong.

DAY 6   How It Looks in Real Life

Women who stay in abusive situations often hope against hope that somehow he will change.

The cycle goes something like this: Tension builds. He is moody, irritable, critical, silent, sullen. She attempts to nurture him, agrees to stay away from family and friends, keeps the kids quiet, cooks his favorite meals, withdraws when she can, and feels like she is walking on eggshells.

Finally, an abusive incident occurs. He verbally attacks with increased psychological abuse. He humiliates her, accuses her of being crazy, etc. He threatens to assault her, maybe forcibly imprisons her. There may be sexual or physical assault or use of weapons. She tries to calm him, tries to reason, and withdraws even further. She wants to leave, to protect herself and the children, and may or may not call the police or a neighbor.

Then, he begs forgiveness. "I'm sorry," he says, often through tears. He sends her flowers, promises to go to church, or get counseling. He enlists family support. "I'll never do it again," he promises.

So, she agrees to stay, or return, or take him back. She attempts to stop the legal proceedings she may have begun. She sets up counseling appointments for him, feels relieved, happy, and hopeful.

Then it begins again—the tension, the abusive incident, her capitulation followed by the "honeymoon period." Round and round, on and on it goes. Statistics reveal that women usually leave between five and six times before they *really* leave.

It isn't hard to see why. No one wants to feel that they have failed. Her need for success in the relationship is as strong as his. He shows his "dedication" through control and force. She tries to console, comfort, and go way beyond being a good wife, doing whatever she can to make it work. In the end, he hates her for this as well. She seems weaker to him by giving in. The love he wants from her and is trying to force from her simply can't happen. Why? *Because love cannot be forced.*

God doesn't force us to love Him because He knows doing so won't work. After all, He created love. He should know how it can be nurtured—or destroyed. When we humans try to rearrange love—to fit it into our sinful minds and attitudes—the results get skewed. The ultimate effects of this distortion can generate lasting damage. The abuser wants approval, love, loyalty. He wants to be served in a way he never was as a child. He may have seen his own father get "results" by using strong-arm techniques, and he tries them as well.

By design, love cannot be mandated. Love is all about freedom. We're drawn in, not pushed in. Fear, hatred, and control simply cannot do what love does. Love heals. It never purposefully hurts. Abuse is never an act of love.

NOTES

DAY 7   Women in Pain, Women in Action

DON'T STOP NOW!

Lenore E. Walker has written a book entitled *The Battered Woman*. It is recommended reading for anyone facing abuse. The *New York Times'* review on the back of this amazing book says: "Battering is one of the underreported and over-mythologized crimes. It is terrifying in its privacy, its intimate violence, its displaced rage and distorted eroticism. Professor Walker's study suggests that not only is it a crime of the…working classes, but battered women are far more common in the middle-class and higher income homes where the power of their wealth is in the hands of their husbands."

TALK ABOUT IT

Think about starting a support group in your home for women. Begin by inviting those interested in the subject to do a book review, perhaps using the one suggested above, or use these lessons. Make it a safe place and invoke privacy guidelines. Ask questions of each other like:

- What would you do if someone in your church came to you for help?

- What do you think about children (grandchildren) being exposed to training about abuse in their school classrooms?

- Can you create a list of ways your church could help victims?

- Does your pastor address these issues?

- Have you ever been close to someone who was experiencing victimization?

Become active in your church and support the idea of a committee to help victims of domestic violence. Approach your pastor, suggesting a sermon on the subject. Loan him a book if he needs something to get him started. Go online and take a course (they are usually free) to learn more about domestic violence.

AND FINALLY...

Over time, women sometimes learn to be "good" sufferers. Pain becomes a part of life, and they carry on. Some women are great codependents and enablers. But no matter how emotionally unhealthy she may or may not be, there is still no reason for abuse, ever. And there's no good reason for it to continue unaddressed, *ever*.

NOTES

Domestic Violence in OUR Church?

WEEK 4

Types of Abuse

DAY 1   We're Not the First

LIVING WORDS

"Do not envy the man of violence and do not choose any of his ways" (Proverbs 3:31).

BOTTOM LINE

Abuse is not just physical. Other types are equally harmful.

SETTING THE STAGE

The United States Surgeon General has reported that domestic violence is the greatest single cause of injury among U.S. women, accounting for more emergency room visits than traffic accidents, muggings, and rape combined.

Historically, abuse has been seen as physical battering—getting "beat up." Nothing much was said about emotional, religious, financial, and sexual abuse. That is changing. Books, magazine articles, and TV shows are addressing the issues. It's also time for God's children to pull their heads out of the sand and take a look at what's taking place in families all around them. Only through knowledge can the threats be effectively addressed. Only with knowledge and willingness can victims be helped.

How can so many readers of God's Word so lightly pass over abuse that's even mentioned in the Bible? After all, "in the beginning" it was there. Cain killed his brother, Abel. Joseph's brothers sold him into slavery. Jacob's deceitful stratagems on his father, brother, and father-in-law caused much grief. Abraham allowed his wife to be inducted into another man's harem and even denied their marital relationship. Adultery, incest, murder, and jealousy are the norm in many biblical accounts. Seems nothing is new under the sun.

DAY 2   Emotional Abuse

A missionary child was heard asking his parents before a social gathering, "Are we going to go downstairs and pretend to be a happy Christian family again?" Can you imagine how such deceitfulness affects a family assigned to do God's ministry? The confusion is especially great for the children.

When a child is abused by a parent, the boundaries that are crossed create a hugely confusing standard. The child comes to believe that such a life is normal, even if it's painful. So it is with Christian families who "play" Christianity. They look good and act good and when they arrive at church, all their little soldiers are impeccably lined up, dressed, and powdered. No one will ever know. In the child's mind, everyone else lives the same way. That's just the way it is with parents. People hurt each other, but church helps, right? We're happy because we *look* happy. Really?

Let's take a peek into one such Christian home on Sabbath morning. The alarm never gets a chance to ring because Father gets there first. Mother quickly follows. She knows what's coming. She has done her best to prepare breakfast the night before, but Dad's favorite egg dish can't be prepared ahead of time. She slips on a housecoat and heads for the kids' rooms. Danny, age 13, was out until 10:00 p.m. last night with church friends. Waking him isn't easy. George is 8 and he isn't roused much more quickly. Little Jenny, 4—the sweetheart of the family—has already bounded out of bed when she heard her mother coming down the hall.

Mother thought she had all the clothes ready but one shoe is missing. Precious minutes are spent searching for it.

It's highly important to Father to be on time. He is the head elder on the platform this morning. He makes a beeline for the boys' bedroom and finds them still snuggling with their pillows. Barking orders left and right, he soon has the boys on their feet. With demeaning comments about their hair and bad breath, he sends them into the bathroom. He's only slightly nicer to little Jenny, who shyly hopes for a hug that she never gets. Mother slips Jenny into her neatly ironed dress, snow-white socks, and freshly shined shoes, then hands her a wet washcloth for her face. Before they have a chance to emerge from the bathroom, Father is pronouncing his displeasure that the beds aren't made.

The car becomes a tomb. Dad is angry that they are three minutes late, and he rails. No dessert today! No going to friends' homes! And certainly no TV tonight! But, one thing is certain. When they exit that car at church, they'd better be smiling.

Mother is reeling from her earlier dressing down about incompetency and laziness, but she once again plasters on the smile, lifts her chin just slightly, and enters the vestibule. She's thankful that her husband will be on the platform today.

This is emotional abuse.

NOTES

DAY 3   Financial Abuse

Never heard of financial abuse? See if this rings a bell.

Betty has been working for the ten years of her marriage. Peter believes he, and he alone, is the head of household and should handle all financial affairs. Betty has been absent from work only twice, during the three weeks following the births of their children.

Betty's paycheck is automatically deposited in "their" bank account—an account in Peter's name only. Peter's name, not Betty's, also appears on the house and the car. Betty takes the bus to work and has strict instructions to be home no later than 5:30.

Betty receives an allowance at the beginning of each month. She receives grocery money (which is never enough), and bus fare for the exact number of trips she will be taking to get to work. She has to ask for anything else on a case by case basis: clothes for the boys or herself, club or school dues, gift offerings for church activities other than what Peter takes care of monthly, and any other incidentals. These are funded only after Betty carefully explains what is needed and why.

There is a life insurance policy, but it is in the boys' names. Gifts for birthdays, Mother's Day, and Christmas are rare for Betty, and usually end up being a five dollar bill jammed in an envelope with no card. Peter is being "wise" and saving for something big. That something big comes soon enough, when Peter finds a motorcycle he likes. Their savings, which would help tremendously toward school expenses, goes into that expensive toy for Peter. He never discusses the purchase with Betty.

Monthly tithe and offering gifts to the church go into an envelope with Peter's name on it. Once a month, Peter gives Betty a list of checks to write but not sign, paying bills that come in. She has no idea how much they owe on the home or cars, or how much is in the bank. Peter believes, as the head of household, finances are his business.

Betty has become numb to the situation. She feels like a slave in her own home. She works hard at a grocery store, but never sees the results of her labors. Peter has convinced her she can't handle money, and only he can make their family financially secure.

This is financial abuse.

DAY 4   Religious Abuse

Nancy grew up in a very conservative home. She was taught that her father's word was law, and that God expected her to obey, no matter what. When she was 21, her father chose a life mate for her—a young man from the same conservative community. They were married before the first kiss.

The young man, Stephen, had also grown up in a very conservative home and was taught that the religious tone and direction of the new home was his responsibility and that his wife was not strong enough to carry any of that load.

From day one, Stephen told Nancy every religious move to make. She was to spend an hour in prayer upon awakening. She was to walk three miles after she fixed his breakfast and was to complete all household chores by 10:00 a.m. At that time, she was to visit those less fortunate in the neighborhood, taking them baked goodies from their meager store, rain or shine. God required it. Stephen required it.

When their first child arrived, Nancy was declared unclean for one month. There were rituals to follow to reinstate her to his bed. The same was true with the second and the third children, all within three years. Her duties were to dress, teach, and care for those three little ones without the help of Stephen. His job was to work. Every weekend they attended several church services, and were never late. God would be displeased.

> **" EVERY WEEKEND THEY ATTENDED SEVERAL CHURCH SERVICES, AND WERE NEVER LATE. GOD WOULD BE DISPLEASED. "**

If Nancy's cheeks were flushed from working in the heat, Stephen would declare that she was wearing makeup and must go in and wash it off. Long dresses and heavy stockings were always to be in place so no man could look lustfully upon her.

Stephen's father faithfully continued to remind Stephen of his place as the man of the home and of the requirements of God's law. Stephen unendingly passed on those requirements to Nancy. He honestly felt he was fulfilling his role as a good husband. He also experienced an exciting and addicting flood of emotion every time he ordered his family in "God's way," as he put it.

When the boys were in their teens, Nancy left. She had loved Stephen, but could no longer be forced to love a God who was so arbitrary, vengeful, and vindictive. She could no longer be married to a man who chose to emulate that kind of God.

This is religious abuse.

NOTES

DAY 5   Sexual Abuse

Georgianna dreamed of a beautiful wedding after Rob swept her off her feet. She just knew she had found her soul mate.

They dated only three months and she lost her virginity the night they became engaged. That sexual encounter created a degree of sadness for Georgianna, as she believed in waiting. But Rob had rather forcefully talked her into it with the excuse, "We're getting married anyway!"

During the honeymoon, Rob began to be brooding and moody and would disappear for hours. When he would return to the beach house, Georgianna was forced to have sex in ways that she had never known about. But she thought it must be perfectly normal since they were married. It was difficult to get used to the multiple times a day routine and soon she was exhausted.

Georgianna was not allowed to work. "I will be the bread winner," Rob announced. She was to remain at home, keep it spotless, and be there and ready for him whenever he showed up. What he meant was, she should be ready for sex even at lunch time, almost every day of the week.

Rob liked erotic toys, and many times Georgianna was glad to see him go back to work so she could treat her uncomfortable body with a warm bath or medicine. It seemed to get worse as the months and years passed.

When Georgianna tried to talk to Rob about their love life, he would become angry and tell her she had no say in the matter—that the Bible says she is to "submit" to him and she'd better do it or else! He would not have a disobedient wife! And furthermore, she was not to discuss their love life with anyone, including (and especially) her mother. There would be severe consequences if she did.

This is sexual abuse.

NOTES

DAY 6   Health Care Neglect

Robie had always been a sickly child. She had tried hard to recuperate during her high school and college days by working out and eating the best she could. But despite her efforts, she was always thin and had multiple health issues. No one, she thought, would ever want to marry her.

She was wrong. Bill took a liking to her during her freshman year in college. That summer, they married.

Bill was a very intelligent young man and soon moved up in his profession. Money was not an issue. However, when Robie became ill the summer after their first child was born, Bill said he was tired of her always being sick and that she needed to just get over it. He refused to take her to the doctor. She was losing weight she could ill afford to lose. Finally, when she dropped to ninety-eight pounds dripping wet, a friend literally snatched her away and took her to the hospital.

Robie was diagnosed with a liver ailment which would need treatment and medications. Bill began to ignore her completely when it came to getting prescriptions filled, keeping doctor's appointments, or going for prescribed treatments. She had to rely on friends or family members and couldn't always get help when she needed it.

Bill insisted that she still do all the housework and food preparation, since she was a "lady of leisure" and didn't have to work. There were days when she spent eight hours in bed, her rest times tucked around meals and other duties in the home. When she was 32, Robie was put on the liver transplant list. She wasn't able to wait long enough and passed away a year later. Bill was so angry he didn't even attend the memorial.

This is health care neglect/abuse.

NOTES

DAY 7   Abuse of Self

DON'T STOP NOW!

Domestic violence has become a leading cause of injury and death for women worldwide. Twenty percent of all women are physically or sexually abused in their lifetime. This violence causes more death and disability for women aged 15 to 44 than cancer, malaria, traffic accidents, or war.

Abuse of self is a huge side effect of growing up in a demanding and demeaning environment. The angry words of parents continue to echo in the mind of the adult: "You clumsy idiot. Can't you do anything right? You're worthless. There is no hope for you!"

It takes much practice to develop a "nurturing parent" voice to take the place of those acrid slaps to self-esteem. Wrongly labeled as "conscience," victims allow those past messages to be played over and over in their minds, denigrating the beautiful worth Christ has bestowed. It's just another effective tool of the Archenemy, the Devil.

But God provides the antidote. "Whatever is true, whatever is honorable, ... just, ... pure, ... lovely, ... commendable, ... think about these things" (Philippians 4:8). No matter what darkness we've experienced in the past, our Heavenly Father invites us to change our pattern of thinking, and concentrate on what's good about us— and about Him. We have the power—with His help—to transform self-abuse into self-awareness. We may not be perfect, but we are children of the King!

TALK ABOUT IT

- How is it even possible to change the facts about abuse within our own churches? Where would we start? Who has the power to put that change in gear?

- Why should it matter to me? My family is OK (I think) so why should I bother?

- Couldn't this become a dangerous topic if we dig into it too much? What if I find that I was abused as a child, or that I am being abused in my marriage now?

- Where would I turn if I felt these things were true?

- Is it worth rocking the boat in my church to bring all this up?

- How can I begin to apply what I have learned to my own life?

- Could there be things I am doing that are abusive?

- Am I abusive to myself?

AND FINALLY...

Perhaps it's time for us to think: "Now that I know more about abuse, perhaps my opinion or outlook on church life has changed. Could a whole new avenue of service be opening up to me?" A good place to begin that journey is to start being honest and open about yourself and your relationships with others. Ask God to help you see the truth, even if the truth is unpleasant.

NOTES

Domestic Violence in OUR Church?

WEEK 5

Man's Far-Reaching Role as Husband and Father

DAY 1   Love Face to Face

LIVING WORDS

"God's answer to man's need was to create woman, one who could be a suitable helper (Genesis 2:18). The Hebrew word used here is one that literally means 'face to face.' That is, God created one with whom man could have a face-to-face relationship" (*Toward a Growing Marriage,* Gary Chapman, p. 57).

BOTTOM LINE

Man is to be a partner, protector, and provider—not a dictator.

SETTING THE STAGE

No one can really say unequivocally what God thinks, what He means, or what He requires. Face it. Human writings are, at best, man's interpretation of what he believes God said, thinks, or commanded. We can find much evidence throughout the Bible, in nature, and among life experiences that offers compelling evidence that God is not what Satan has made Him out to be. Ever since the war in heaven, Satan (Lucifer) has used lies and deceit to create an image of God that is, in reality, his own image. And his ultimate goal was—and is—to create distrust of God within man. If he can do this, he wins the battle for man's attention.

Today, after thousands of years of degradation, man is in a much better position than Adam and Eve to see what evil truly is. This does not, however, seem to put modern man in a better position to keep from sinning. Through the third and fourth generation and beyond, the tendency in the human heart is to create havoc. Without Christ's redeeming power, man is hopeless.

How then, does a man fulfill the plan for lasting love and unity that God has for him? How does he fulfill the obligation created for him by his family—his wife, his children, his home, his job, even his aging parents—all without becoming overwhelmed?

Some, not understanding God's plan for families, may even ask: Why does a man need marriage to carry out those obligations? Can't he provide love, companionship, sex, a home, social acceptance, and financial security without a marriage certificate?

THINK ABOUT IT

Can any relationship truly be one of unity without God? How can the husband bring God into the relationship and make it a beautiful thing?

NOTES

DAY 2   The Husband's Need for Direction

Take out a pencil or pen and a note pad, and begin to write down ideas as to how we can create a loving environment for our families. Then beside each idea, write how that effort can be short-circuited, or how selfishness can destroy that endeavor. Let's look at some examples. Idea: Spending quality time with each child. Short-circuit: Working long hours and missing important events in a child's life. Idea: Speaking encouragement to a discouraged wife. Short-circuit: Ridiculing a spouse for losing a job. List a half-dozen or so.

Ken Nair has written an incredible book called *Discovering the Heart of a Man*. He maintains that God actually ordained a type of spiritual leadership that the wife can receive only from her spouse and that it helps her in her own search for spiritual maturity. He believes that if that leadership negatively affects the wife, their relationship—and their spirituality—will suffer. He, like other authors, notes that most men unconsciously operate on the premise that leadership is found in strength, which they translate into domination or control rather than the ability to sense one's own spirit and the spirit of others.

Mr. Nair writes that when a person operates from an improper premise, the outcome is all wrong. The same is true of understanding God. If we see him as angry and wrathful, and we work from the premise that we are to be like Him, the outcome is wrong. While we can forgive many improper actions by husbands and fathers—just as we do with women who also grew up believing wrong things about our Heavenly Father—does this excuse abuse? No.

Does being very knowledgeable concerning the Bible necessarily make a man a spiritual leader? No again. Nor does being a charismatic speaker or being able to keep his family "in line" mean he's on the right track.

Mr. Nair lists the qualities that a true leader of the home will possess: love, patience, peace, joy, a forgiving spirit, being available, understanding, conducting himself in a manner that gains and maintains his wife's trust, and proving that he maintains a strong commitment to God.

DAY 3   Male Leadership Gone Wrong

The flip side of a husband's role might require a life partner to surrender mind, emotional being, will, choices, goals, dreams, and desires. How would that play out in daily life? Consider this story, set in first person for clarity.

My name is June. Frank and I were married rather young, but when I married him, I had pretty big dreams. I wanted to be a nurse practitioner. He was not as ambitious, but he went on to own his own business and do rather well. However, when I wanted to apply to college to continue my studies, he told me I couldn't because it wouldn't look good for me to have more education than he.

As children began to come along, I became more and more simply the woman who raised Frank's children. Even my attempts to volunteer in a medical institution were denied me, as Frank said I needed to be at home to keep things going for him since he was so busy with his business.

He *was* busy. I rarely saw him. Neither did the children. I learned to just give in each time we had a difference of opinion about anything, because it was easier than arguing, and I knew I couldn't win.

At first I wanted to run away. Then I think I just lost touch with reality and decided to let life happen. I know it changed me.

I felt lost. I just wish he would have been willing to compromise and allow me to grow in my own sphere. I think my love for him would have grown instead of dying. It's hard to love someone who has his thumb on your heart all the time.

How could June have more healthily reacted to Frank's misconception about leadership and helped him grow as a husband and father? To begin with, she could have set some healthy boundaries and let him know that she would fulfill her duties as wife and mother, but she would not give up her dreams.

If Frank was not an abuser, he might have respected her for setting goals and letting him know she would not give up. If he was addicted to control, the level of force might have escalated, showing her who was boss.

June always had choices, but she may not have recognized them and the fear of the unknown may have kept her there trying to keep the peace and raise a family.

Ken Nair clarifies why some men never know what their wives need. It can be because of her silence, jeopardizing any chance that she will reach out to him toward oneness.

It's true that many Christian women suffer in total silence, believing this is what God wants of them. Nair reminds such women that even if their husband criticizes the validity of Christianity because of their frailty, God can handle it!

NOTES

DAY 4   Can Women Change Men?

QUESTION

Can women change men? Short answer: NO.

Despite all the popular songs to the contrary, and despite the occasional situation where the influence of one draws another into a better lifestyle, the greatest percent of relationships bring two people together who stay the same throughout that relationship.

There are certainly things a wife can do to encourage a husband. Let him know when he does something that pleases you—something that uplifts you. Tell him when you are proud of him or how he manages his business or life. Encourage your children to let Daddy know how special he is, not just on Father's Day. Show him with eye contact, special gifts, praise in public, one-on-one time, and a hundred other ways that he is the man of your dreams.

But if the wife is the only one doing these things, sooner or later, they will stop. Sooner or later the critical phrases, curt orders, under-the-breath sneers, eye rolling, and time spent away will tell a greater story than words ever could.

God created women to respond. But just as God's law is love, He knows that we have a choice of whether or not to respond to Him. The same holds true for a marriage relationship. Once again, love cannot be forced. Love draws. Love softens. Love creates. And only God's *love* can change a man.

When a woman demonstrates a love to her husband and children that is not co-dependent or dysfunctional, it opens a door for God's love to change that man and child from the inside out. Unfortunately, once again, the percentages are not so good. When a man is entangled in the addiction of control it is very difficult to break free even if true love is staring him in the face. Not impossible. Just difficult.

When things are not going well, it may be necessary for the two parties to heal separately. They should get separate help/counseling to identify the reasons that abuse has been used and accepted for so long. God can reunite if He sees fit—and if both parties are willing. But healing must come first.

One of the myths of abuse in families is that children and/or the wife are better off with an abusive spouse than alone. If a house is on fire, a person will have to remove him or herself in order to survive. The same is true in an abusive household. In fact, staying may inhibit the abuser's ability to heal or find help.

THINK ABOUT IT

Can you imagine any situation in which a wife is better off staying within an abusive household? Do children respect a parent more for staying through abuse than for separating the home for safety sake?

NOTES

DAY 5   The Child's Perspective

From the perspective of children, Mother and Father are there to love, protect, and entertain. When things become abusive, their little world is turned upside down. Nothing makes sense. The people they trusted have begun to do hurtful things.

Since they have nothing to which to compare life, they begin to believe that their life is normal. If the abuse extends to them personally, it will affect them even more. The damage done from being present where their mother is experiencing domestic violence may be as difficult to correct than as if the abuse was against them.

Since woman was built to respond to man, much of her personal value can be derived from whether or not she feels accepted and loved by her husband. In turn, that woman may or may not have the courage to be what she needs to be—what she *wants* to be—for her children. When the spirit is being sucked out of her, there is little left to give, even to her kids.

Thus children *always* suffer in domestic violence cases. They either live in fear of seeing a parent hurt, or are scared they will be left by one or both caregivers.

Most unfair of all, they often believe that the problems exist because *they* are not being good enough—it's *their* fault. If parents split, they take that blame on themselves and will need careful guidance to remove that idea.

A wise caretaker—school teacher, babysitter, relative—can sometimes explain to that child that the troubles are not because of him or her. But since most violence issues remain under cover at home, rarely will that support become available.

If you are in a position to see this child in action, some signs may be apparent. There may be changes in behavior or school performance. There may be learning difficulties not attributed to specific physical or psychological causes. The child may be overly compliant or act out repeatedly. That child may stay as long as possible after school, not wanting to go home. And those sweet faces may show signs that they are fearful of something bad happening. The best thing you can do is simply be their friend.

DAY 6   It Takes Two

Before we continue, a word of caution. If there is no history of abuse in the relationship, and a woman or man suddenly exhibits abusive behavior—verbally and even physically—it would be well to facilitate a medical examination to be sure there are no health problems that might be causing the changes. Diabetes, runaway blood pressure, food allergies, and brain tumors are among those medical dysfunctions that can cause behavioral changes.

Courtship can be a great time to evaluate the patterns of a possible mate. A short temper, argumentative spirit, impatience, emotional pattern changes, nervousness, etc. are all reasons for concern. Many have married believing they can change a mate once they are married. It simply doesn't work that way. The chemicals created during courtship put a person on his or her best behavior. If there are obvious problems before marriage, no doubt they will be much worse as life takes hold after the honeymoon.

Even in the best of relationships, an objective view of life is different through the eyes of a man than of a woman. It takes tremendous desire to study each other, understand each other's minds and how they work, and to create a rewarding relationship. When either partner chooses to push his/her own agenda without caring for the other person's emotions, separation happens. Damage is done and repair is difficult until one or both parties choose to operate under God's law of love, and are willing to admit their own weaknesses. The fly in the ointment appears when one partner is determined to rule the other no matter what.

Mike and Gayle Tucker, co-hosts of the TV program "Lifestyle Magazine" do a delightful job of walking couples through building (or rebuilding) a marriage in their "Mad About Marriage" seminars. They explain that there are big and very destructive issues that weigh heavily on a marriage—some easily recognized and some not so much. Couples often struggle unsuccessfully to get anywhere toward an effective relationship, not even realizing why they are thwarted. The Tuckers have successfully helped couples identify and deal with many of these issues. Unfortunately, it's hard to get an abusive spouse to attend any such seminar. But it is worth a try!

What should parents do if they are watching their young adult become engaged to an obviously controlling person? Is there a way to address the situation which makes it understandable to the person in danger, or will the chemistry override reason? How does a parent best support that person who may choose to go ahead with an unwise marriage?

NOTES

DAY 7   A Look in the Mirror

DON'T STOP NOW!

Check out these excellent resources:
- *Toward a Growing Marriage* by Gary Chapman
- *Discovering the Heart of a Man* by Ken Nair
- *The DNA of Relationships for Couples* by Greg Smalley and Robert S. Paul
- *Jesus, Your Heart's Desire* by Mike Tucker

TALK ABOUT IT

If you are a husband, think about how you can dig deeply into the needs of your spouse. Like any dysfunction, domestic violence can be portrayed on a scale of zero to off the charts. Somewhere on that continuum each of us can find ourselves.

Whether you are a member of an abusive household or not, spend some quality time looking at where you sit on that scale. Evaluating personal relationship techniques, how you show other family members you care, whether your heart is in tune with their needs, and how willing you are to learn more of what they need— all of these are very valuable for opening your eyes to habits or attitudes that may be short circuiting your relationships.

Every relationship can be improved, even the good ones. Make it a routine activity to spend some time evaluating your own interaction with those you love. And if God opens your eyes to abusive things you may be doing on a regular basis, get help. Don't delay.

Start with your relationship with God. Make sure you know who He is and that you understand how He uses His power. Then, if you need professional help changing something in your home life, don't hesitate to get it.

AND FINALLY...

It is said we never stop learning. Education is lifelong. Fathers can be the solid support that gives families life. Or they can— perhaps through improper family education—become the tool that tears families apart.

Domestic Violence in OUR Church?

WEEK 6

Passing It Down

DAY 1 Love Face to Face

LIVING WORDS

"If a parent is abusive in any way—if he overeats, overworks, or overdoses anything to the neglect of his family—that behavior will affect his children's lives for years to come...being attracted to dysfunctional people, medicating their emotions with compulsive behavior, or becoming addicts themselves" (*Never Good Enough*, Carol Cannon, p. 19).

BOTTOM LINE

Eye-opening concepts may bring us closer than we might wish to realizing our abusive behaviors.

SETTING THE STAGE

All too often, we Christians have hung our hats on belonging to a strong group of people headed for heaven. We believe that our *own* salvation is the most important issue, and *secondarily*, we hope we can bring friends and family with us.

Salvation, of course, is what God wants for us all. This is so evident in Christ's sacrifice on Calvary. But should my own salvation be my main goal? Is heaven, eternal life, and endless rewards where I should place my focus? Was that Christ's main focus when He came to earth? Or was He willing to take the chance of never seeing His Father again in order to save someone else? With Jesus, it was all about others. How should this knowledge guide us as parents or family members in our interactions with our family and friends?

Luke 9:24 reminds us: "Whosoever would save his life will lose it, but whoever loses his life for my sake will save it." Reciprocal giving—the "circle of life"—is such a beautiful concept. Let's see if we can understand it a bit better in this week's lessons.

DAY 2   Human but Teachable

Keep in mind as we delve into this area of study that we all come short of the glory of God. It's not the occasional deed or misdeed that determines the direction of our lives. The same holds true of abuse. Abuse is a pattern of behavior, not the occasional act for which we turn immediately to God and say, "I don't want to be like this. Please change me as You see fit. I can't do it alone."

During this process of change, there may be a need to ask forgiveness of others affected by our actions. Through these instances, earthly friends and family can eventually learn to know each of us as a loving, non-abusive entity in their lives. If forgiveness is never sought and change never comes, true abuse may well be present.

Consider this insightful quote: "People bring all of the debits and liabilities incurred in childhood into their adult relationships and impose them on their mates and children, and the children pass them along to the next generation.... It is possible to be a committed Christian and still be dysfunctional (unable to function as God intended).... Becoming a Christian does not negate the law of cause and effect. If a child is wounded, he will bear the scars" (*Never Good Enough*, Carol Cannon, p. 19).

There is probably not a parent anywhere who, when face to face with an adult child, doesn't wish he/she had done something differently in the raising of that child. We're notably human! Thankfully, God can even use our disabilities in teaching our children the right way to live if we're honest and open concerning them. Children usually know instinctively whether we have their best interest at heart, despite our blunders. They know whether love is the motive, or selfishness has taken over.

Therein is the core of control. Do we teach, restrain, advise, punish, or discipline in order to mold this child into someone who will honor us, or is our primary goal to show that young mind how God has lovingly allowed mankind the freedom to choose and love? A question we should be asking ourselves repeatedly as we interact with our young ones is: What will they think of God when we are finished shaping their young lives and they reach adulthood?

THINK ABOUT IT

Which would you love to hear your adult child say in a heart-to-heart talk with you? "Dad (Mother), there's one thing for sure. I will never be like you! My life and my family will be different. I want nothing to do with your brand of religion." Or: "Thank you for showing me the heart of God—how He loves me unconditionally, protects and guides me, and gives me the gift of His commands—and for explaining how the natural laws He created are for our joy and well-being. Thank you for letting me be me as I matured. You made sense, ultimately, although I may not have understood everything every time. I love you for being my guiding light until I could understand how to let God guide me."

You may never hear exactly those words. But to watch that child mature into a loving, sensible, spiritually-aware adult is reward enough.

NOTES

DAY 3   Unity in Diversity

"Train up a child in the way he should go; even when he is old he will not depart from it" (Proverbs 22:6).

One author's view of this text says that "the way he should go" refers to a child's natural bent or inherent talents. Other views suggest that they will come back to the church if they stray, and fervent prayers go up to that end. Meanwhile, we live in a "do what I say, not what I do" society. It's no surprise that many children get confused about what a parent wants.

Have you ever heard someone say that they have tried their whole life to get the approval of a parent? No matter what they did, they were never as good as an older brother, sister, or even a friend. "I'm not the son my father wanted," one might say. Many adults push themselves into a profession or a religion trying to prove to their parents—who may not even still be alive—that they measure up. Much emotional energy is wasted in this "less than" mind game.

Listen to this amazing quote: "One of the greatest encouragements of the Bible is seen in the diverse natures of the men Jesus called to be His disciples—James and John, the sons of thunder; Peter, the impulsive one; Andrew, the friendly one; Philip, the practical man; Nathanael, the visionary; Matthew, the accountant. And yes, even Judas, the businessman who betrayed Jesus. Each was unique. Jesus never made comparisons. He dealt with his disciples as individuals and loved them as they were. He respected their differences" (*The Child in Each of Us*, Richard W. Dickinson & Carole Gift Page, p. 19).

So how does all this fit into the domestic violence or child abuse scene? It's a matter of control. If I believe that, as a parent, I must mold my child to be like me—or maybe much more perfect than me—and if there is a misunderstanding about what God's Word has instructed us to teach our children, could that translate into control? Could our methods be so anxiety-ridden (If I don't do a good job, God will not forgive me) as to create an environment where healthy growth is impossible? Absolutely. It's the control that is abusive, even though the acts may not seem harsh. With a smile on their face, many individuals have covertly strong-armed another. With a pleasant voice, one can give another no choice in a matter. Consider the motive as well as the tenor of the act.

There are so many ways to be abusive. Satan has certainly seen to that. Yes, some acts are obvious—physical, sexual, etc. Others are harder to identify.

THINK ABOUT IT

How do I go about reviewing my own motives and actions to ensure I am not unknowingly using emotional or physical control on those in my life? How do I change?

NOTES

DAY 4   Parental Responses

"But children are so willful!" many parents (and teachers) moan. Yes, we are all born with a propensity to selfishness—me first, survival of the fittest.

In *Could It Be This Simple?*, Dr. Timothy Jennings book about the human mind and how God designed it to be used, the author talks about the will. Dr. Jennings writes: "Everything depends on the right action of the will because it is the part of mind that chooses. Consider when Satan took Christ to the pinnacle of the temple. The devil tempted Him to throw Himself off from there. Satan could not push Christ off—Christ had to make the decision Himself. The same thing applies to our own conflict with Satan. He can never force the will. Rather, we must *choose* to surrender ourselves to his suggestions." Jennings reminds us of James 1:15 about how our desires gives birth to sin, and when full-grown, sin gives birth to death. "It does not matter whether or not you actually carry out the action. If the will says yes, but you never perform the act, the mind is still damaged, the conscience bruised, and the reason clouded" (p. 88).

Remember the story of the little boy who was told, in no uncertain terms, that he must sit down? His response was: "I may be sitting down on the outside, but I'm standing up on the inside!" The point is that whether we carry out a threat to a person or not, our attitude is often all it takes to damage both our own soul and theirs.

So, what was Christ's modus operandi concerning disobedient adults when He was here? Did He use force? We might remember the story of His cleansing the earthly temple with whips and overturned tables (see Matthew 21:12-16). Look closely. Did He hit/hurt anyone? Weren't there those who stayed, unafraid because they saw His love and intervention?

Or, how about the scribes and Pharisees incident recorded in Matthew 23? "Woe to you...hypocrites!" Even then, using endless love, He tried to wake them up.

Think about Mary Magdalene, Peter, the soldiers who came for Jesus, the ten lepers. There were whole towns healed and forgiveness freely given to those who put Him to death.

Christ came to show us the Father. "I and the Father are one"

(John 10:30). "I do not say to you that I will ask the Father on your behalf; for the Father Himself loves you" (John 16:26-27). "If you knew me, you would know my Father also" (John 8:19).

THINK ABOUT IT

Wouldn't it be an incredible honor for some young person to emulate you; to want to be like you because it makes sense, not just to please you, but because the you they see matches their concept of a loving God? Jesus and His Father are the ultimate illustration of God's natural law on which the universe was designed to run. It's the law of love. Anything less disconnects us from the source of power and life.

NOTES

DAY 5   Be in Charge!

How do we pass on to future generations the picture of God as it should be? Let's use the concept of exercise and good health as an example. Professionals—and those who have made appropriate changes in their lives—will tell you: the best way to influence your kids or others in your life circle is to *be the change*. No one listens to someone who doesn't live their truth. It's usually easy to see through the dealings of someone who talks the talk but doesn't walk the walk.

We're not talking about becoming critical of others. God can use a person despite their body type, weight, health, or the personal and often hidden battles they fight such as habits. If He couldn't, He'd be limited to a very few of us to carry the Good News!

But how incredibly strong the temptation is to ignore words and deeds of someone who can't uphold their own lifestyle with appropriate life-giving concepts. Think about your own dealings with yourself. Would you trust yourself to help others if you are bogged down with addictions, fears, doubts? Only as we give those shortcomings to God for healing can we become willing to share with others what He has done for us. Learning to be the change, to be the loving self that God has created us to be, is perhaps the highest calling to mission service on earth. We can talk until those proverbial cows come home. But it's true—actions always speak much louder than words.

We must also keep in mind that even actions can be forced. Trustworthy actions are a natural outgrowth of understanding who God really is, and believing that He gives us the freedom of choice. The more we study God's true character, the more we become like Him. The converse is also true. If we are focused on God as mean, vindictive, and even vengeful just waiting to punish us, we will become like that.

A 6-year-old boy asked his grandmother why there were water droplets on the leaves early in the morning. It hadn't rained. (He asked "why" about a lot whenever they took nature walks). Her answer, along with a simple explanation of how it works, was "Because God made it that way." It wasn't long before that child was answering his own question. When he'd ask why, he'd quickly add, "Oh yes, I know. It's because God made it that way. Right Grammy?"

What a thrill to guide the mind of a child to the incredible loving power of God and the beautiful gifts He gives us. This world is ugly on so many levels: destruction, war, hatred, greediness, fear. But when we look on God's incredible gifts that are not yet totally erased, we find ample evidence concerning who He is and how He longs to interact with us.

NOTES

DAY 6   Why Children Become Abusive

QUESTION

Are there some effective ways to pass on the knowledge of God to a younger generation?

Beginning at birth, how do we assure that tiny baby that he or she is loved? One concept of child rearing suggests that a child is willful from birth, and when they cry for a period of time, the child's will must be broken. A hand should be placed over their mouth and nose until they stop crying. Then the hand is removed. This is repeated, until the child realizes it has to stop. That advice is given for newborns in some circles.

But that's abuse, clear and simple. Just when that tiny life is needing assurance that they are cared for and nurtured, instead they are placed under abusive control. That parent is breaking the very will that the child will need later to make wise choices. It is not for parents to break a child's will, but the privilege of a parent to guide that tiny will into adulthood, teaching self-control in a healthy manner. God forbid that we begin a child's life with such treatment! Does God deprive that parent of the very air they breathe until they do exactly as He wants?

Let that little one grow up in the knowledge and experience that they are loved unconditionally. As they are given age-appropriate chances to use self-control with explanations of why it works well, the little one can healthfully mature. Take that tool away, and the result is a co-dependent, perhaps addictive personality that cannot see through pain to grasp for healthy growth.

Children learn to avoid abusive behaviors through such avenues as appropriate loving, dedicated parenting, educational institutions and teachers, grandparents' influence, friends, pastors and church affiliation, spouses, and others. We even learn from our children and grandchildren. Yes, even old dogs can learn new tricks, as the saying goes. Perhaps it isn't salvation through senility— quitting all the bad stuff because it is just too much effort. Perhaps life experiences finally solidify us more and more, restructuring us into the type of person we have spent the most time observing.

Since children learn 90 percent of what they will ever know—

personality wise—in the first few years of their lives, their observation of adults—either parents or other people in leadership—is vital. Each moment, each hour of contact with a young life is a molding experience.

THINK ABOUT IT

What are two things you can personally do next time you have an opportunity to interact with a young person that will point them to the true and loving character of God?

NOTES

DAY 7 Molding Young Minds

DON'T STOP NOW!

Increasingly, there are presentations on domestic violence or child abuse on TV and radio or given by organizations, awakening churches and pastors. Take every opportunity to increase your knowledge in this area. Get a God-centered book from the library or the bookstore. Make the acquaintance of someone who is a leader in this field or who has been through the experience of abuse and is willing to share. Be brave enough to ask a child in your circle of influence what makes them believe in God (or not believe). Share with them your concept of a loving God and how that has changed your life.

TALK ABOUT IT

So how can what you learned this week benefit you and those around you? You may well want to re-read this week's lessons if you can't answer that question. Take time to underline in color those things you believe can change you and help a child understand God. More importantly, spend some serious time in the Word, strolling through nature, and observing life experiences to discover the truth about God.

Continue the earlier suggestion of taking an unmarked Bible, reading a chapter at a time, and making notes at the end about what this tells you about God. Try using your new paradigm about God to understand how He dealt with people in Christ's day, and how He deals with us today.

God is not changeable. What He did back then, He does today. Truly, as the song says, "It is no secret what God can do." But it is not always easy to see. We have matured in a world that has misshaped the picture of our Heavenly Father into one we misunderstand and then fear. It takes time to overcome the ugliness that our Adversary has placed on God's image. A wonderful spiritual reward is waiting for anyone who spends the time to get to a better understanding of who God is and who He desires us to be.

THINK ABOUT IT

Could our learned concept that God demands obedience—that He is a "jealous" (like earthly jealousy) God and will punish us if we disobey—be the catalyst for passing on inappropriate behavior?

AND FINALLY...

Families/children are molded by their understanding of God and what He requires of them. Even those who deny the existence of God are controlled by some thought of a "Higher Power" and what he/she/it expects of them. Let's take the time to be sure we have an appropriate picture in our minds.

NOTES

Domestic Violence in OUR Church?

The Bible's Standard for Relationships

DAY 1   Biblical Clarity

LIVING WORDS

"Wives, submit to your own husbands, as to the Lord …. Husbands, love your wives, as Christ loved the church and gave himself up for her" (Ephesians 5:22, 25). "And it is my prayer that your love may abound more and more, with knowledge and all discernment" (Philippians 1:9).

BOTTOM LINE

The misuse of Bible texts can totally change the look of a functional relationship.

SETTING THE STAGE

Why does it matter what the Bible says? It would be easy to answer that with a traditional response. But we must go deeper.

Either we believe God is trying to get through to us—to give us guidelines that will ultimately enrich our lives and our eternity—or we believe He has arbitrarily given out a set of dogmas to control our existence.

What we think definitely changes how we act. So, when we finish this week, we can review the realities of our lives and what we might wish to adjust for a better quality of life—adjustments that will benefit both us and others.

Philippians 2:1-3 reads: "So if there is any encouragement in Christ, any comfort from love, any participation in the Spirit, … complete my joy by being of the same mind, having the same love, being in full accord and of one mind. Do nothing from selfish ambition or conceit, but in humility count others more significant than yourselves."

It seems Paul was hoping for unity of heart and mind. We might do well to approach this advice with some interest.

DAY 2   Bible Evidence

The Bible is not always easy to understand. Perhaps you, along with many others, have voiced the wish that it had been written in a numbered sequence of "do this and live" lists. Think again. God is not out to corral us into being good little children who know all the rules and never step outside the boundaries. If He were that kind of ruler, He would have created us as puppets, "loving" Him because we were programmed to do so.

Instead, God has allowed mankind to be inspired with stories of how God treats His children—all of them. Surely there are texts that make God look a bit arbitrary. Still, God gave freedom to the writers—and later the translators—to state things as they believed they should be stated. Rather than criticizing or throwing out the proverbial "baby with the bathwater," we should view the Bible as a whole, including all sixty-six books.

When we are walking through those stories and begats and written laws, we will do well to ask ourselves repeatedly if we are slipping back into the "I must or else" attitude, or if we have learned to listen for the true voice of God in those writings.

Ephesians 5 is often used by abusive spouses to prove that the wife or husband should obey explicitly, and that they have no rights. That abuser obviously didn't read on. Nor, perhaps, did the victim.

Have you noticed that there are many religious organizations—multitudes of churches with slightly different names and concepts? Have you ever asked why? Could it be that many have grabbed onto certain texts and created a religion around them without reading on? Noticing the divergent religions of the world, we tend to gather proof texts around us in an all-out attempt to show the world that we are right and that our way is the only way to heaven. In the very act of doing so, we demean Christ's sacrifice and attempt to remove the gift of freedom offered by Jesus' own hand.

There is only one way to salvation and that's through Calvary. Was it because God required blood to be able to forgive? Or could it be that God and Jesus (one in purpose and unity) knew that unless one of them came to earth to show us the plan, we wouldn't know how to respond to it? Wouldn't it make sense that without knowing God's purpose for us, we would be lost? By becoming one of us,

Jesus was able to show us the Father and lay out the incredibly sensible plan they had for us—to live for eternity in the originally intended fashion.

Do you trust the Bible? Does it make sense to you? Or do you have to constantly "lay things up on the shelf to understand later" because of viewing it as a rule book instead of as a light shining in the darkness, revealing God's true character?

NOTES

DAY 3   Get Wisdom

When the Bible is taken "word literal," most things seem to have been written as a black and white directive. Let's review:

- Cain killed Abel – literally.
- David had an affair with a woman and had her husband killed – literally.
- "Blessed shall he be who takes your little ones and dashes them against the rock!" (Psalms 137:9). Do we want to be exactingly literal in this case?

Have you ever misunderstood your spouse or someone else speaking to you? Certainly. We can misunderstand the Holy Word, too. One thing is rock solid sure. God does not teach confusion. The bottom line message of the Bible is that He is all powerful, but He does not misuse that power or use force. Love cannot be forced, or it ceases to be love. That is God's natural law. So if we are getting mixed messages from the Word (and we often do), it is due to our paradigm, our sin-tainted ability to understand, our knowledge (or lack thereof) concerning the words used.

Salvation does not hinge on us having all the right texts or the right understandings exegetically speaking. Life is not a graded quiz where, if we pass, we go to heaven. God is looking for a people who understand and trust Him and who will truly want to live with Him for eternity within the boundaries of His incredibly healthy natural laws. He wants to restore our lives back to how they were originally designed to be lived: no pain, no sorrow, no sickness, no hatred or selfishness. Though He never forces us into it, everything He does is designed to draw us to that more healthy way of life.

Let's look then, at how a man and woman can come together in a relationship that fulfills God's plan for them here on earth.

One Christian author believes that we can have a bit of "heaven on earth" within our families as we become better acquainted with God's purposes. Most marriage partners desire that very thing as they stand at the altar on their wedding day. Unfortunately, over fifty percent of marriages fail. Perhaps this is why so many young people choose to live together without the certificate of marriage. However, those relationships can fail as well. There are no guarantees. But are there some concepts and beliefs that would tend to stand a couple in good stead relationship-wise? Consider these beautiful texts:

"Get wisdom; get wisdom; do not forget, and do not turn away from the words of my mouth. Do not forsake her, and she will keep you; love her, and she will guard you. The beginning of wisdom is this: Get wisdom, and whatever you get, get insight" (Proverbs 4:5-7).

"Search me, O God, and know my heart! Try me and know my thoughts! And see if there be any grievous way in me, and lead me in the way everlasting!" (Psalm 139:23-24).

"A man who is kind benefits himself, but a cruel man hurts himself" (Proverbs 11:17).

So, how can the Bible-reading Christian home have percentages of abuse as high as non-Christian homes?

NOTES

DAY 4   Tips for Youth

Max Lucado, speaking of church politics in his book, *No Wonder They Call Him the Savior*, writes: "How many leaders have saddled their pet peeves, drawn their swords of bitterness and launched into battle against brethren over issues that are not worth discussing? ... 'May they all be one,' Jesus prayed. One. One faith, One Lord. Not Baptist, not Methodist, not Adventist. Just Christians....No hierarchies. No traditions. Just Christ" (pp. 126-127).

Take it down to the family—or a couple. Would anyone deny that it is only when two people get on their "high horses" and stay there until they are proven right, that under those circumstances division occurs? Or, what if only one person feels a certain way and the other gets tired of fighting and becomes a "shadow person"? You have the perfect circumstances for abuse to occur. Whenever one human tries to control or manipulate another on an ongoing basis, abuse takes place. Whether it is done by a church leader or a home leader, it's still abuse. When the one being controlled feels that there's no recourse, no hope, no joy, they are victimized.

Perhaps that person needs some professional guidance on how to set healthy boundaries. Perhaps the situation is resolvable, improvable. Perhaps not. But when either physical or emotional safety is an issue, intervention is needed. That is only possible if the affected party is willing to be helped.

TAKE A LOOK

So what does a functional family / couple look like? Sometimes we study dysfunction so much that we forget to talk about what is normal. Let's see if we can shed light on normalcy.

- **Father:** Provider, protector, encourager, lover, willing to listen and learn, spiritual guide, forgiver, planner. You probably can add your own favorite attributes to this list.

- **Mother:** Nurturer, responder, teacher, caregiver, sweetheart, homemaker or professional or both, idea creator. Again, add your own.

Are there telltale signs of future abuse potential that young people should notice when launching into a relationship? There certainly are:

- Possessive behavior, keeping partner away from friends or family
- Pushing partner into a sexual relationship
- Anger or displeasure at how things are done
- Non-respect for parent of the opposite sex
- Lack of responsibility in any level of their life or relationship
- Difficulty telling the truth
- Cruelty to animals, children, or peers
- Critical or vindictive actions
- Improper use of Bible texts or Christian ideas
- Anything uncomfortable on a continuing basis

That's just for starters. Awareness comes slowly for two young people whose chemical magnetism is in full swing. Wise parents can help their offspring by explaining some of this before they are in the middle of it. Many leaders in the field are realizing that education concerning domestic violence really needs to begin in grade school! Certainly, it is a delicate subject, but one that really needs to be voiced early to prevent generation after generation from falling into the same traps.

NOTES

DAY 5   Twisted Words

We know this: the devil is indeed the Father of Lies. We also know God is truth. He doesn't just *tell* the truth, He *is* truth. And the truth is, God is love.

We can make it difficult, but the bottom line is that love can solve so many of our human problems, needs, and necessities. It can melt hatred. It can lift us out of hopelessness. It can create an atmosphere wherein spiritual growth is boundless.

The word "love" has been misused, twisted, and its true meaning obliterated. Like many words, it can have multiple meanings. "Love" can mean lust, deep appreciation for inanimate objects, feelings of desire, and tenderness. We will not fully understand love until eternity, and then it may take thousands of years for it to soak in.

Within the true meaning of that word is encased so much: loyalty, trust, friendship, forgiveness, faith, feelings of good will, unconditional caring, etc. Perhaps there ought to be a class every year for students on what love actually means, and how to experience the real thing. But, just as with parenthood, there are no classes. We're simply expected to "get it."

1 Corinthians 13 (KJV) calls it "charity." Charity is so important that, if we do not have it, we are "nothing." Charity, or love, "is patient and kind; love does not envy or boast; it is not arrogant or rude. It does not insist on its own way; it is not irritable or resentful; it does not rejoice at wrongdoing, but rejoices with the truth. Love bears all things, believes all things, hopes all things, endures all things. Love never ends" (1 Corinthians 13: 4-8). That pretty much cancels out most human love, but it so beautifully describes our Heavenly Father. And, it gives us something for which to strive. Home would truly be heaven on earth if these concepts were firmly in place.

Just as God in Christ reconciled the world to Himself, not counting our trespasses against us but desiring for us reconciliation, the role of each spouse—the privilege really—is to pass that love on; to make available to those around them the reconciliation offered to them through our Savior. What a difference this would make if we were living like nothing was more important than being reconciled, and being a reconciler (not a fixer). We would not be doing this in order to be saved, but because we recognize we are a forgiven and loved son or daughter.

THINK ABOUT IT

If you could go back in your own marriage (or other relationships), what things would you like to be able to rethink and perhaps change? Can you forgive yourself as Christ has forgiven you? If not, why? Are you willing to address those issues and find forgiveness so you can grow into the man or woman Christ desires you to be? It is never easy to face our own need to change.

NOTES

DAY 6 Heart Tenderizer

QUESTION

What does it take to change a hardened and dysfunctional heart into a heart of flesh, one capable of offering freedom and true love? We will not pretend to take the professional approach, using psychology or psychiatry. But let's spend a moment or two finding the help offered in Scripture.

Galatians 5:17 tells us that the desires of the flesh are against the Spirit, and vice versa. It makes it very hard to do what you believe is right. We find ourselves in hot water over and over again because of this war in our bodies and minds. Verse 22 says that "the fruit of the Spirit is love, joy, peace, patience, kindness, goodness, faithfulness, gentleness, self-control; against such things there is no law." We are further admonished not to provoke one another.

Many marriage enrichment weekends include exercises on how to use these fruits with each other with some degree of effectiveness. We are encouraged in the next chapter to bear one another's burdens, and by so doing, we fulfill the law of Christ. What law is that? The law of love. We must remember in all the techniques we might deploy, memorizing and acting out suggested routines in a relationship will only be temporary at best. A change of heart must happen before unity is a reality.

Do you recognize that you are the workmanship of God? Ephesians 2:10 states: "For we are his workmanship, created in Christ Jesus for good works, which God prepared beforehand, that we should walk in them." What an incredible honor to be called "the workmanship of God." Let the knowledge of your belovedness sink in. Know that this incredible God is your Creator, your Father, your Savior. Then ask yourself if, with that kind of worth, you want to do anything else except live in the graciousness and peace of Him who gave you life. Share it with your spouse, your family, your friends. Be the person you were created to be and bask in God's gift.

That kind of living is what changes lives. That kind of knowledge is what unlocks the fears and meanness of someone who has, until now, known nothing but force and controlling techniques. Then and only then can the victim and/or the abuser be healed. The desire has to come first.

How excited the heavenly hosts must be to see someone in that predicament come alive, realizing their heavenly worth and allowing God to heal him or her. There is much joy when one comes to the fold, no matter from what past. "But grace was given to each one of us according to the measure of Christ's gift" (Ephesians 4:7).

No exceptions. Healing is available to all!

NOTES

DAY 7   Getting Practical

DON'T STOP NOW!

Read Corinthians, Galatians, Ephesians, and Philippians. You'll discover that the One who has begun a good work in you is faithful to perform it. Here you'll learn that your love can abound more and more and you can be filled with the fruits of righteousness. Remind yourself that love never hurts another in your hands. Forgive yourself. Ask others to forgive you when necessary, and kneel at the feet of God and request healing. It will not be withheld.

Discouragement will try to short circuit the struggling addict or abuser. Don't give up! Fall again at His feet. Grab hold and don't let go. When you feel separated from Him, it is not because He moved. Learn to love your own body/self as Christ does, so that the admonition to love your spouse as you love your own body will make sense.

TALK ABOUT IT

Get practical. If you are an abuser (maybe you were unaware before), ask yourself how to become more aware of your problem. Think: Can I ask my spouse to help by reminding me when something feels uncomfortable? Should I go for professional help? Are there books I can read? Should I talk through past issues with parents or siblings and resolve things that might be fueling my fires? When is it good to talk to the pastor? Ask yourself: "Do I *really* want to change, or do I just want out of the limelight for now? Do I trust myself?

If you are the victim, you need to know: Am I safe right now? How far back does the abuse go? Is he/she getting help, or are cycles repeated with worsening results? Are my children safe? Is there anyone to help me? If I am interested in what is most redemptive for all involved, what action will help stop the cycle of abuse and what choice will I make? Am I willing to set boundaries and follow up with changes if they are not observed? Have I felt I did not deserve anything but abuse, and is that why I am staying? What action on my part cooperates with God for greatest healing—continuing the cycling of injury and abuse, or stepping back to stop the destructive cycle, even if that means getting separate counseling and therapy?

AND FINALLY...

Pastors do well when they include 1 Corinthians 13 in the wedding admonition. Love (charity) is unmistakably *the* building block in any relationship, especially the home. Christ—and the Heavenly Father He reflects—is our supreme example of how to treat each other.

NOTES

Domestic Violence
in OUR Church?

WEEK 8

How Children Learn to Be Abusers

DAY 1   Self vs. Others

LIVING WORDS

"God is in control ... He certainly is. But here's the vital point ... the very fact that God has any living enemies at all, informs us that He has chosen to exercise His sovereignty by granting real freedom ... risk[ing] ... freedom rather than ruling with a dominating control" (*An Endless Falling in Love*, Ty Gibson, p. 40).

BOTTOM LINE

Earthly husbands can safely pattern themselves after God's loving provision for us.

SETTING THE STAGE

Have you ever wondered how a sweet little child becomes an abuser? What could possibly cause a man (or woman) to "need" to be abusive? Where does that training begin?

When a man and woman pledge their love at the altar, what is it that changes later to create a distasteful relationship? Again from Ty Gibson's book, *An Endless Falling in Love*: "Relationships in which there is a mutual exchange (a circle) of positive giving and receiving—respect, trust, integrity, kindness, sympathy, and forgiveness—tend to yield mental and emotional confidence, self-respect, motivation, productivity, and creativity, equating to positive mental health. Relationships in which one's focus becomes centered on self rather than others—deceit, manipulation, cruelty, hate, sexual perversion—produce a sense of isolation, insecurity, guilt, low self-worth, suspicion, phobia, and a lack of will to create, produce, and even live. Hence, mental breakdown" (p. 24).

Once again we see that natural circle of love. Though perverted by Satan, that circle is God-designed and still available to those who are connected to their Heavenly Father. When that life-connection is broken, the mental health (character of the person) is damaged. And when the damage is not repaired, the relationship progresses in a downward spiral which may very well end in death for one or both.

DAY 2　The Image Destroyed

Think back about your relationship with your own earthly father. You may have wonderful memories of working alongside him, learning the tools of his trade, camping/hiking trips into the mountains, horseback riding, or fishing in clear streams. There may be explicit memory videos of the warm, welcoming smiles you received as you came home from some activity, and you may have some excellent advice stored up from his wisdom. Or (unfortunately for many of us) we cannot conjure up good memories. Rather, there's scorn, "never-good-enough" looks, yelling either at us or our other parent. Anger may well up within our hearts at the memories we've tried hard to stuff out of reach.

Is it safe to say that our picture of our Heavenly Father may, if we are honest, remind us of our earthly father? Have you ever said to a business partner, boss, or spouse: "Don't put your mother's face on me. I am not your mother (or father, etc)."

Imagine how difficult it is for God to reach us once Satan has misconstrued the meaning of fatherhood or parenthood. Punishment, harsh words, selfish control have clouded many a child's heart toward his or her God. They believe He is just like an earthly parent or guardian.

God's greatest manifestation of love—the core of who He is— shows up dramatically in His creation of man. Yet the image of Himself that God created in man has been perverted and literally destroyed over the centuries. Repeatedly, Satan chooses the family unit in which to play out this destruction.

"The thief comes only to steal and kill and destroy" (John 10:10). Despite the original design for parenthood, evil has been able to so disrupt that plan that some have found themselves addicted to harshness and abusive actions. The beauty of a solid, nurturing relationship and selfless love has indeed been stolen, and death and destruction are the result. Even if the physical body does not die (more than 30 percent of all women's deaths by homicide are at the hands of a family member), the heart/soul may well find some relief in emotional death. The victim puts one foot in front of the other each day, hoping not to upset the apple cart, praying that the very God whom they think requires them to stay will give them the strength to stay. This exacting "god" may even look a bit like their spouse.

THINK ABOUT IT

How can we as a church, as Christians, find ways to change this? Where does Christian counseling come into play? Can pastors, from the pulpit, effectively influence what goes on in a home? Should women (or men) who are victims be able to find safety within the church family?

NOTES

DAY 3   Family Dynamics

Parenthood is tough. Finances, spiritual life, relationship issues, home maintenance, keeping up a good reputation; it's a huge and time-consuming job! But when proper connections are made early on with a child and/or spouse, and trust is established, there can be much joy and internal peace. Parenthood can be rewarding.

But all too often the dark side of parenthood rears its ugly head. "He who fails to find me [God's wisdom] injures himself" (Proverbs 8:36).

John was raised in a family with twelve other children in the early 1900's. The iron rod of his father was combined with the necessity for all hands on deck in making a living in the Kansas wheat fields. Between the dust bowl and just plain hard times, it's understandable that the eight other boys played a huge role in John's development as a man.

Their advice about women was not always wise. When he married his high school sweetheart, a combination of exacting religion and the need to survive caused John to display a heavy hand in their relationship. His little wife had to dress, act, cook, clean, and bear children in his prescribed manner, and it wasn't always easy.

The woman lovingly swept out the sod house's dirt floor and washed little white, hand-sewn feed sack dresses for their three girls in the washtub with water drawn from the well with her own hands. It wasn't the hard work that finally made her send him away. It was the heavy-handed control. This little mother may have been young, and she may have been a minister's daughter, but one thing she knew instinctively: she was losing her identity, and it wasn't comfortable. She'd drive the tractor, dirty her hands in the garden, and make her own clothes, quilts, and even his overalls. But she stopped at losing herself in his shadow.

One day, even though she did not know where the next meal would come from, she sent him away. "Enough!" she said.

Thankfully, this young father's heart learned far more in those 18 months of separation about the need for freedom of choice than he'd learned in 18 years from his family of origin. Finally, the relationship was restored and the family reunited. Yes, God can and does work miracles. But why does it not always happen that way?

Both partners have to be willing to identify, examine, and deal with issues. Those issues have to be worked out on "safe ground." Both victim and abuser must want change, desire God's re-creative power, and be willing to partner with Him. Without this, you have an inescapable stalemate.

THINK ABOUT IT

Is it always because of a misunderstanding of God that abuse happens? What are some signs within church families that there may be issues? Can healthy families become examples within the Christian community? Where should training on how to treat each other really begin: grade school, high school, or college?

NOTES

DAY 4 Life Commandments

In his book, *A Child Called "It,"* Dave Pelzer graphically lays out the ultimate abuse by a mother. His descriptions cause agony in the hearts of any feeling reader.

Satan has seen fit to assure as many children as possible that there is no such thing as parental love. The recently telecast story of a young lady held in the bedroom of her captor's home for ten years shows that even a father finally reunited with his daughter can still lay the blame on the child. This particular child was abducted at age 14 after being groomed by a man in a leadership role. Was that father perhaps the reason this young woman was vulnerable? Yet, in the end, he laid the blame on her.

If we were to get the full and true stories of all church members, perhaps we would see that it is not all that uncommon for children to grow up believing their worth is very small to zero. There may not always be stories of physical abuse—cigarette burns, being locked in a closet, drinking lye water, etc.—but the insidiousness of words, looks, and actions within the "beautiful" home may well be eating away at self-worth, the ability to trust, and one's view of God. Christian children get "set up" for defeat just as easily as non-Christian children!

See if you recognize any of these stinging clichés from your childhood: "Straighten up. If you don't stop crying, I'll give you something to cry about." "You're too old to act like that!" "Why don't you act/dress/speak like 'so-and-so'?" "Your brother can do that—why can't you?" "I'm sick and tired of you. Go to your room." "There are just so many hours in my day, and you are ruining several of them!" "Give me that toy. You don't deserve to have *any*!" "Why can't you obey me just one time?" "Pretty is as pretty does." "If you touch that again, I'll wring your neck!" "Don't you lie to me, you little scoundrel." "You're getting on my last nerve!"

Not exactly confidence-building, right? Where does it begin, this feeling of having to control something? If a child's only view of God is by watching a parent, it isn't hard to see why gradually that child becomes an adult that fears or even hates God because he/she is so very tired of having to live up to unreal expectations. Why are we so surprised to see runaway children? Yes, even runaway adults!

Tomorrow we will examine the interesting transition that takes place as we mature—that of creating the "invisible parent" inside us based on how our actual parents treat us. It makes sense. If our parents treat us with respect and teach us self-confidence and trust, that "inner voice" will continue to guide us in right paths when we leave their counsel and protection. If not, that voice becomes our worst enemy. Parental abuse easily turns into "self" abuse.

NOTES

DAY 5   Let This Mind Be in You

In the informative book, *The Child in Each of Us*, by Dickinson and Page, we learn that our inner voice is likened to an answering machine tape. You record a greeting, and unless you change it, that same message plays over and over.

So, let's say you spill a carton of milk. You immediately hear that "critical parent tape" inside you, playing: "You clumsy idiot, can't you do anything right?" But, the authors say there's hope. You can learn to place a nurturing parent message alongside that critical one, and then learn to turn off the bad tape. New Age, you say? Well, let's look at what God's Word says about it.

"Finally, brothers, whatever is true, whatever is honorable, whatever is just, ... pure, ... lovely, ... commendable, if there is any excellence, if there is anything worthy of praise, think about these things" (Philippians 4:8).

Philippians 3:3 further states: "Glory in Christ Jesus and put no confidence in the flesh." Sounds a lot like learning *not* to believe the "fleshly" untrue "critical parent" messages that we give ourselves many times a day. We could learn to rejoice instead.

"Have this mind among yourselves, which is yours in Chris Jesus" (Philippians 2:5). Using the *What Would Jesus Do?* slogan, we realize that our precious Savior would not have depreciated Himself. He knew He was the Son of God. We share the same divine genetics!

We'll call this type of degradation "self abuse." Trust is the biggest issue for children and adults who have been abused. It makes sense that we might not even trust ourselves, as those critical "parent tapes" play. Christians sometimes call that voice "conscience." There is some question as to the accuracy of that label. Is it possible that Satan has found a way, even through well-meaning parents, to place totally false words into our heads about ourselves, about others, and even about God?

"Victim" is the word used for those who suffer from domestic violence, child abuse, or any other controlling relationship. Child abusers rarely, if ever, admit their sin. Incest isn't disclosed outside the family. Children are groomed for abuse and seem to see no way out. Yes, "victim" may well be totally appropriate in many cases.

But, we can let those around us know that there are choices, safe places, and that they don't deserve abuse. Can victims become free to choose? Yes!

THINK ABOUT IT

Listen to your internal voice. Is it nurturing? Encouraging? Uplifting? (Pure? Lovely?) Take a day or even one hour to write down every message you give yourself. Are you shocked at the negativity?

Now, ask yourself: Have I been taught to "down" myself, to negate my own worth, to be "less than" in my own eyes? Am I to lift everyone else up, but pull myself down? What makes me less a child of God than my neighbor? What is the difference between false modesty and true Christ-like humility? Does my desire to downgrade self have anything to do with what I think God does to me?

NOTES

DAY 6 The Dirty Dozen

TAKE A LOOK

Let's take a look at actual physical things that we may not have recognized in the past as abusive to a child. We'll call them "The Dirty Dozen." Feel free to add things to this list that you may have experienced and now recognize as abuse.

1. Obsessive tickling. Being held down, not stopping when they are out of control.

2. Biting back (or hitting back). Young children who bite may be cutting teeth, or they may be plain mad. Find a better way to deal with it than to confuse the issue!

3. Arm twisting. "Say 'Uncle'...." (this might happen between siblings).

4. Hiding from a child in a store to let them feel the fear when they haven't obeyed your instructions to stay close.

5. Requiring a child to sit perfectly still during worship that is lengthy.

6. Making a child stand in the sun on a hot day—facing the outside wall—for punishment.

7. Using a child for adult medical care (like giving a shot) at a very early age.

8. Hurting or mistreating a pet in front of a child.

9. Using spiritual quotes/texts in anger to show the child how "evil" they are.

10. Taking children on scary rides when they don't want to go to "toughen them up."

11. Allowing children to watch scary movies or listen to adult TV programs that involve violence.

12. Leaving young children in unattended diapers for extended periods of time.

We might add using food as punishment or reward. Think of the likelihood of food-related disorders in adulthood due to these highly questionable tactics.

Of course there are many others. The principle here is to think how the child will react—out of fear or out of love—and choose your actions appropriately.

There are rare situations which may look momentarily abusive such as snatching a child from traffic or away from a bare electric wire or out of the jaws of a biting dog. They may not always understand your sudden action. But when you can calmly explain your action, let them know why you did what you did. It can be a huge boon to the bonding process.

The bottom line is this: If we abuse a child, it is very likely he/she will be an abuser or a victim when they get into an adult relationship. Rarely will someone be strong enough to fight the generational influence and find health in their spiritual and emotional life, especially if the abuse has been horrific.

THINK ABOUT IT

Can grandparents be influential in how their grandchildren are raised? How does one keep appropriate boundaries and still do this? If you are a leader at church and you see childhood behaviors that scream "abuse at home," what do you do? What do you not do? Do you have a right to do anything?

NOTES

DAY 7   Recovery's Beginnings

DON'T STOP NOW!

Dialog about abuse toward children is never comfortable. However, the bravery it takes to learn more about it, address it, and be prepared to help when possible is highly valued. Two books written by Dave Pelzer may prove helpful: *A Child Called "It"* and *A Man Named Dave*. Another good resource is *When Dad Hurts Mom: Helping Your Children Heal the Wounds of Witnessing Abuse* by Lundy Bancroft.

Only you can decide at what volume and speed you acquire and read the resource materials. But be aware that if there is some resistance on your part, there may be a reason—a reason that needs sorting out and addressing. Take your time, but never stop becoming equipped with knowledge.

TALK ABOUT IT

Perhaps the most difficult place to start recovery is with a family member. If a person feels there has been some abuse in the family, but can't put a finger on it, a heart-to-heart talk with a sibling might be good. Secrets do finally come out in many cases. The saying is: "You can't heal what you don't reveal." The reveal needs to be done with a safe person in a safe place, so choose wisely. But, if there are issues you can't explain, and fear of even finding out the why, find someone to talk to. It may be a professional who guides you through the process. It may be as simple as talking to that sibling.

Stuffing the past in a corner and covering it with addictions (workaholism, religiosity, perfectionism, alcohol, drugs, sex, etc.), will not make it go away. The results will be a "leaking sideways" in your life—acting out in ways that speak loudly of issues that need to be addressed. It happens no matter how far down things are shoved. Physical health is also often damaged.

Most importantly, our loving Heavenly Father can heal the hurts of the past and present. Many times He uses humans to accomplish this. In His presence is where we must stand. Ask Him for the strength to open your heart and mind to His healing, and then trust His methods.

AND FINALLY...

Like the spelunker readying himself for the cave—ropes, headlamp, extra batteries, clips, and just the right shoes—this week we have positioned ourselves at the beginning. We'll learn more along the way concerning the effect of domestic violence on children. Read on.

NOTES

Domestic Violence in OUR Church?

Does God Abuse His Power?

DAY 1   My Identity in Christ

LIVING WORDS

"My identity as Abba's child is not an abstraction or a tap dance into religiosity. It is the core truth of my existence. Living in the wisdom of accepted tenderness profoundly affects my perception of reality, the way I respond to people and their life situations" (*Abba's Child*, Brennan Manning, p. 72).

BOTTOM LINE

How I view myself in God's eyes plays a role in how I treat others.

SETTING THE STAGE

Studies of Christian men reveal that one of their greatest fears is that they will be "found out." They do not feel that they are as strong and viable as others picture them. They feel like a fraud (in business, etc.)

Women, truth be told, face some of the same troublesome feelings, especially in motherhood and/or their chosen profession. How we deal with these feelings of inadequacy shows up in a multitude of ways. Some are obvious. Sometimes we "leak sideways," wanting to get messages across, but not wanting to come out and say it. Anger and fear are very interrelated. Ask any aging person who fears what their future holds and they will certainly second this.

But, more life adjusting still is our fear of who God is. Is *He* a fraud? Christians say He's loving. But, is He *really*? We hear that He designed an ever-burning hell into which He will throw those of us who don't please Him. Does He control every happening in my life until I feel shoved and prodded and abused? Why do so many people see Him as angry? Is He fearful that we will find out who He is, or does He wish we *would*?

DAY 2   The Effect of Prejudice

The quote from *Abba's Child* is part of a book that effectively brings us face-to-face with our own identity, and makes us take a long look at the source of our conclusion. Has our life plan been laid out by a human, or are we feeling the joy of being God's loved child?

Brennan Manning is a defrocked Catholic priest (but still a Catholic) who has gone from university professor to ditch-dwelling drunk to recovering addict to proclaiming his belovedness (and yours) in Christ Jesus. He shares how his humanity still clings to the illusion that he must be "morally impeccable, other people must be sinless, and the one I love must be without human weakness." He admits to a gnawing hunger for vindication, and that his identity as Abba's child "becomes ambiguous, tentative, and confused." Manning's life experiences have taught him that "we are sons and daughters of the Most High and maturing in tenderness to the extent that we are for others—all others—to the extent that no human flesh is strange to us, to the extent that we can touch the hand of another in love, to the extent that for us there are no 'others'" (*Abba's Child*, p. 72).

Growing up in a childhood of prejudices, bigotry, false beliefs, racism, and homophobic feelings, Manning came to understand that all of these are defense mechanisms against loving, and that "denial and repression are in fact what gives them power." He reminds us that our neighbor is the one to whom we give compassion.

Manning tells the story of a time when he and his wife Roslyn were on Bourbon Street and a young, smiling girl named Susan approached them with a flower and asked for a donation. She was from The Unification Church. She was a "Moonie." "Obviously she had two strikes against her—first she was a pagan who did not acknowledge Jesus Christ.... Second, she was a mindless and vulnerable kid who had been brainwashed by a cult." Brennan said to her, "Susan, I deeply admire your integrity and your fidelity to your conscience.... You are a challenge to anyone who claims the name 'Christian.'" He remembers: "Roslyn reached out and embraced her, and I embraced the two of them. 'Are you Christians?' she asked. Roslyn said, 'Yes.' She lowered her head and we saw tears falling on the sidewalk. A minute later she said, 'I've been on my mission here in the Quarter for eight days now. You're the first Christians who have ever been nice to me. The others have either looked at me with contempt or screamed and told me that I was possessed by a demon. One woman hit me with her Bible'" (*Abba's Child*, p. 76).

That day, young Susan saw God in action. She saw/felt love and acceptance, and she was drawn to it. Christ promises that if He is lifted up, He will draw men to Himself. That day on Bourbon Street, He was lifted up.

NOTES

DAY 3   Does God Abuse?

Our question for this week is "Does God abuse His power?" There is no doubt that God is all-powerful. We've established that by now. The question is, did He abuse that power or use it wrongly?

The stakes are not small. Manning talks about how man was able to use the "genius of legalistic religion—making primary matters secondary and secondary matters primary." He reminds us of the Sabbath—the day that was to be a blessing and a joy to God's people, and how it was made into a legalistic burden with rules and regulations.

It was these same legalists, doing all "the right things" that ultimately killed Christ. And then they hurriedly took Him down off the cross before Sabbath so as not to tarnish that day; the day that God Himself had given to them as a blessing.

God could have stopped the crucifixion. Christ could have come down off the cross and slaughtered everyone, starting over with only people who would treat Him right. Why didn't He? Because that act would have been using His power to force obedience. How could the rest of the universe trust Him to be a fair God if He arbitrarily went about choosing who lived and who died? His real mission was to show us two things: 1.) the awfulness of sin and who the Father of Lies really is, and 2.) the love of God, and what He's really like. Jesus came to give us the facts, so we could choose whom to serve. The only way God could do that was to allow Satan to accomplish his awful deed—the death of His beloved Son, in whom He was well pleased. The only way for us to understand the depth of His love was to see the whole plan played out.

Yet, time after time, we hear beautiful Christian voices proclaiming that God will do awful things to those who do not love Him. In some circles, there is no *everlasting* burning hell, but God will still punish some longer than others as they deserve. He will vindicate the saints by torturing the wicked who tortured the saints.

Jesus said much to try to clear the air. Still, we do not see it. Manning states that the image held by many about God necessarily locks people into a theology of works, because they have to keep the law impeccably in order to "induce God's love."

Does this mean God is like that? "A vague uneasiness about ever being in right relationship with God haunts the pharisee's conscience. The compulsion to feel safe with God fuels this neurotic desire for perfection. This compulsive endless moralistic self-evaluation makes it impossible to feel accepted before God. His perception of personal failure leads to a precipitous loss of self-esteem and triggers anxiety, fear, and depression" (*Abba's Child*, p. 86).

There it is. The pharisee in us is the fraud!

NOTES

DAY 4   The "Pharisee" in Me

It's interesting—revolting, really—that we have attributed to God things we would *never* do to our own children!

Say you have five children, ages three to nineteen. They are all dear to your heart, but a couple of them are always wearing you down, causing trouble. As a parent, even if you are not the quintessentially patient parent, would you even *think* of destroying those two because they do not correctly "represent" you? After all, they don't fit into your perfect plan. They have disappointed you.

You would *never* do that—and not because you don't want to go to jail. Your love for those "black sheep" is strong enough to generate continued support, prayers, and probably financial assistance as long as you see it is helping. You hope and pray for their lives to ignite with the love of God. You desire only happiness for them.

But God, we say, is not that way. He's worn out, waiting for us to "get it." And sooner or later, He will take the lot and throw them into hell forever and ever, keeping them alive so they will be tortured. Some, we say (like Hitler and Stalin), deserve it. But what about your son or daughter? What if they have been turned aside by false teachings in school or home and never seem to understand who God really was? What if they are standing outside that heavenly gate? At that point, what do you want God to be like? Wouldn't you cry for mercy for your child? Is it OK with you to serve a God who arbitrarily chooses whom to save and whom to torture for eternity?

Using the pharisee in contrast to Jesus, Brennan Manning shares this: "The power games the pharisee plays, gross or subtle, are directed toward dominating people and situations, thereby increasing prestige, influence, and reputation. The myriad forms of manipulation, control, and passive aggression originate in the power center....The pharisee within has developed a fine radar system attuned to the vibrations of any person or situation that even remotely threatens his position of authority" (*Abba's Child*, pp. 94-95).

Two dysfunctional people will, like Velcro, be attracted to each other even from across the room. A power player has a sixth sense about who will play into his game. He watches for the very person who will become vulnerable to his control, initially being totally enamored with his presence, only too late to discover the evilness. It doesn't matter that he eats the right things, wears appropriate clothing, gives to the poor, or is even in leadership within a chosen church. If the propensity to control is there, abuse is the outcome, sooner or later. Christ did not have that propensity. He was tempted like we are, but He did not give in. Even in the garden and on the cross, His will remained in sync with His Father's.

THINK ABOUT IT

Do you serve God because you dare not do otherwise? Or have you asked Him to heal you and fit you into His plan?

NOTES

DAY 5   Biblical Beliefs Misunderstood

Make no mistake. Death happens. Decisions will be made, and eternal death will be the result for many. Destruction is inevitable. And although we will have to wait to see exactly how it plays out, we can trust God's decision-making process.

We do have much evidence of who God is, and who Satan is, and what techniques they both employ. So, why do we continue to attribute to our loving Heavenly Father those "acts of God" and end-time events that we should be hanging on Satan's shoulders? How effective that old serpent has been in convincing us that God is the villain. How sad it is that we've swallowed his lies—hook, line, and sinker.

Why does it matter what we believe about God? Well, the fact remains: If we believe that God is like Satan has made Him out to be, and if we believe we are admonished to "be like Him" in every way, that definitely affects our spiritual life, our actions, and our relationships. And what about our salvation?

Again from *Abba's Child*: "Faith in the present risenness of Jesus carries with it life-changing implications for the gritty routine of daily life.... And yet it may happen in these most desperate trials of our human existence that beyond any rational explanation, we may feel a nail-scarred hand clutching ours....The tragedy radically alters the direction of our lives, but in our vulnerability and defenselessness we experience the power of Jesus in His present risenness" (pp. 103, 105).

Yes, He can be felt in our daily lives. He can heal us if we put ourselves into the care of the Great Physician.

Have you lost passion in your life? Being aware of Jesus' presence is ultimately and intimately linked to recovering your passion. We can only "be the change" if God changes us, and that happens only when we trust ourselves to His fairness, His freedom-giving, and His power to heal. We can be driven by passion once again *only* when we see hope.

When we allow our addictions to numb our senses (co-dependence, workaholism, control tactics, or substances), our ability and capacity to be Christ-centered is diminished. If we block out our need of passion for life, afraid to put ourselves out there, we will gradually feel apathy and mediocrity in our life. Abusing someone may make a person feel inappropriate passion for a moment, but the damage done is quietly killing both the victim and the abuser.

Victims can gain autonomy from abusive relationships by accepting their belovedness, their worth in Christ Jesus. It will give them strength to protect their children and themselves, realizing that Christ did not say, "Love your neighbor *instead* of yourself," but "Love your neighbor *as* yourself." Giving up one's God-given identity does not glorify Him. God can no more give up His identity than we can stop the rotation of the world.

NOTES

DAY 6 Is God Trustworthy?

QUESTION

Can God be trusted?

"Who would dare to question the integrity of God? Who would dare suggest that God cannot be trusted? Yet with this incredible accusation, the Biblical account of human history begins. The one who raised this charge has not always been God's enemy" (*Can God Be Trusted?*, Graham Maxwell, p. 2).

Maxwell goes on to tell how Lucifer, the "Morning Star," became the Father of Lies (John 8:44). He started with Eve, assuring her she would not die if she ate of the forbidden fruit. The rest, as they say, is history. Are we still wallowing in that lie? Do we still listen to Satan rather than God?

"How often religion has sought to crush man's freedom and deny his sacred right of individuality! How often religion has insulted human dignity, demanding blind submission and belief! All this bespeaks an arrogant and arbitrary God. Is this the truth that Jesus said would set men free? Or are these Satan's lies about our gracious God? Does God desire the obedience of fear or the obedience that springs from trust and admiration for the rightness of his ways?" (*Can God Be Trusted?*, p. 15).

In answer to the "God is Dead" movement of the early 1960's, a song was written. "My God is a Real God" speaks of a trustworthy, authentic entity who is the creator of the world—every tree and flower, a miracle unfurled. And, the song goes: He lives within my heart!

It's no wonder many have become atheists or agnostics, setting aside the very One who lovingly created them. The image of God painted across our world has been one of an arbitrary, cruel, and inappropriately powerful God.

The things that we attribute to Him are nothing less than abusive. He is said to send devastating storms, winds, and floods. We're told that He "needs" the parent of a young child in Heaven more than that child needs him/her here on earth and so He "takes them away to be with Him!" God destroys without reason, and causes disease and destruction. Really?

Everything, some say, comes from God. Where else would it come from? God is all-powerful, right? And yes, in the end, He decides who lives and who dies, and He keeps those alive that deserve death so He can torture them for eternity. What a monster! It seems we owe Stalin an apology.

Still, church signs declare GOD IS LOVE. Preachers proclaim that if you give your life to God, everything else, including your finances, will become wonderful. We print "In God we Trust" on our money, and we speak it in our Pledge of Allegiance. Yet we rail at God for not fixing the problems of church and state. When will we stop talking out of both sides of our mouths?

NOTES

DAY 7 Religious Organizational Control

DON'T STOP NOW!

In *The Myth of a Christian Nation*, Gregory Boyd delightfully lays out a clear picture of how our so-called Christian nation has strayed far from the very principles upon which we believe our founding fathers built it. He reminds us that we are deceived if we think for a moment that we can fulfill the great commission by trying to take control through the power of the sword. The kingdom of the world cannot be made into the Kingdom of God. The only way, Boyd reminds us, that we can win the world for Christ is by people being transformed from the inside out through the power of Christ's love.

TALK ABOUT IT

Isn't it refreshing to find an author grasping the reality that ultimately, force never wins? Despite being programmed as we are through wars and military endeavors to think that force—being the biggest and the best—wins, we can see that ultimately it does not.

Ask yourself: Have our nation's efforts to put an end to war succeeded? We've won some wars but have lost the battle. The battle against evil still rages. We conquer, Gregory Boyd says, only by refusing to place our trust in the violent "power over" kingdom of the world, and must instead make it our sole task to manifest the unique righteousness of God.

When was the real battle won? That's right. On the cross. So, how do we allow His sacrifice to be manifested appropriately in our lives so that the world can see the stark contrast between the kingdom of the world and the Kingdom of the Lamb?

A Hallmark movie, *The Second Chance*. ends with the minister sitting on the roof of his condemned church in an effort to save it. When asked if he was scared, he answered, "I want to learn to fear absolutely nothing but God Almighty." Can you think of ways we have been programmed to believe that we need to *fear* God? How has that word been used inappropriately? I'll tell you how. By taking it out of the realm of "respect" into one of being frightened. This simply puts one more nail in the coffin of our distorted picture of God.

AND FINALLY...

If everything depends upon the right action of the will, it must be highly important for the will to be guided by truth, and ultimately the truth about God. Any departure from seeing God as He truly is and believing the archenemy's lies separates us from the source of life.

NOTES

Domestic Violence in OUR Church?

WEEK 10

Detecting Need Within a Church Family

DAY 1   Heads in the Sand

LIVING WORDS

"Ultimately the blame is widespread for Christian believers worldwide who tend to ignore, minimize and deny the abuse that is rampant in families of faith. Churches provide few resources for victims of abuse" (*No Place for Abuse*, Catherine Clark Kroeger & Nancy Nason-Clark, preface).

BOTTOM LINE

We're getting down to brass tacks this week. Recognition, education, safety, action is our goal.

SETTING THE STAGE

"Maybe across the ocean, but not in *my* church!" "There's nothing I can do. Talking about it just makes it worse." "I have enough of my own problems. I don't want to know about the problems of others."

It's a pretty basic thing, really—loving others. It's God's passion. It should be ours, too. Why is it so hard? Yet week-in and week-out we enter the church doors playing a verbal ping-pong game. "Hi, how are you?" "I'm fine, how are you?" "I'm fine"...and so on. No one really expects the person asked to respond with "Well, I'm not doing so well. My husband beat me again this week and I am afraid for my life. I don't know where to turn or to whom to talk."

Do we ever mean "How are you, *really*?"

What does it take to be aware of the signs of abuse? What is the difference between being nosey and really caring? Won't getting acquainted with this information simply make us paranoid? Am I responsible for fellow church members? Let's address those questions.

DAY 2   Hard Statistics

This week will contain quite a few facts: statistics, experiences, training on how to make a difference. Take the ideas presented here and ask yourself if you have ever seen evidences of abuse without recognizing them. Learn everything you can about the subject. Make reference cards and keep them in your wallet or purse with resource information to give to someone discreetly if they do get honest with you.

First, let's go to the statistics. In the past five years, Dr. René Drumm, Ph.D. and her domestic violence team have not only done heavy research, studying hundreds of church members, gathering surveys in a manner that allowed for complete privacy, but they've also interviewed personally at least forty women who are church members and who were willing to talk about their past abusive relationships. From this research project come the following numbers. You will see the categories first, then the percentage of men and women who indicated that they have experienced that particular kind of abuse in an intimate relationship.

Keep in mind that these figures come from dedicated Christian homes.

- Controlling and demeaning behavior: 61 percent

- Intimidation and physical violence: 42 percent

- Sexual victimization: 26 percent

- Resource deprivation (being deprived of food, sleep or medical treatment): 22 percent

- Potentially lethal actions (beatings, using or threatening to use weapons): 9 percent

Nationally, ninety-five percent of all domestic violence cases reported are men against women, although occasionally it's the other way around. Thirty-one percent of all women killed were killed by a husband or boyfriend. Just to put this in perspective, during the Vietnam war, 58,000 American soldiers died. During the same period, 54,000 women were killed by their significant others. If you compare Christians statistically with these national averages, our numbers are just as high!

Here's another sobering statistic. "Children who watch victimization of their mothers are five times more likely to exhibit serious behavioral problems than other children" (*No Place for Abuse*, p. 37). Physicians in training often use the phrase: "See one, do one." Hands-on learning is very effective. Unfortunately, it is also very effective in the arena of violence. "Normal" to a child is what they grow up with, good or bad. This is not just physical violence, but it applies to emotional, verbal, and sexual violence as well.

So, let us ask ourselves: If Christianity is such a great thing, if we believe all people should believe in Christ, and yet our lifestyle— our "proof" that Christianity works—is still heavily tainted by domestic violence (and by default, child abuse, etc.), how can we expect the world to look on us and want to be like us?

Where are we failing? Do our dogmas create change that is real? Do our organizations represent love in action? When can we expect to belong to an organization into which we really want to bring others, because it is life changing?

NOTES

DAY 3   Christ's Example

"The Lord is my shepherd; I shall not want.... Even though I walk through the valley of the shadow of death, I will fear no evil, for you are with me" (Psalms 23:1, 4). How many victims of abuse have repeated these verses over and over?

How did they arrive at a place in their lives where this was necessary? In movies, books, and real life, we've all seen it—the cryptic advice handed down from mother to daughter: "You made your bed, now you must lie in it. It is your duty to be a good wife no matter what card you were dealt. God expects you to be sweet and loving no matter how you are treated. Just pray more. Claim the promises…"

To clarify, there is absolutely no reason *not* to memorize the wonderful promises and talk to God about an abusive situation. The damage comes when advice like we see here becomes the final "choice" for an abused woman or man. When the person experiencing abuse becomes boxed in with no alternatives, they are abused at the hand of the abuser, but also the misinformed advisor takes part by infusing hopelessness.

The Psalmist David warned of such "advice." "For my father and my mother have forsaken me, but the Lord will take me in. Teach me your way, O Lord, and lead me on a level path because of my enemies. Give me not up to the will of my adversaries; for false witnesses have risen against me, and they breathe out violence.... Wait for the Lord; be strong, and let your heart take courage; wait for the Lord!" (Psalm 27:10-14).

Not even Christ stuck around to be abused and perhaps even killed—disappearing out of a crowd on more than one occasion when harm was imminent. He knew two things: It was not His time, and He knew letting the crowd have their way would not bring people to Him. Only at Calvary, in order to fulfill His mission on earth, did He willingly submit to the final scenes of His earthly life. Rarely are people called to duplicate that brand of submission.

No doubt there are beautiful Christian women who truly believe they are required by God to stay and take abuse. They may well believe that allowing their children to see their willingness to be "sacrificed" will make the children stronger, or cause them to become loving Christians. However, the statistics don't bear that out, nor does reality.

Inappropriate use of texts can create some "life commandments" that haunt us through a lifetime. God offers love and protection and finds ways of getting His message through to those who need it most. We must never depend on someone else's interpretation of Scripture. God's Word is personal. He speaks to us through His Word. If He speaks to you, listen. Just be sure the appropriate "filter" (God's law of love) is in place!

NOTES

DAY 4   Signs and Symptoms

Here's a list to make us more aware of the signs and symptoms of abuse:

- Bruises, bandages, broken bones, recurring bodily damage

- Quietness in groups, especially when spouse is present (head down)

- Never allowed to attend meetings, parties or other group events

- Isolation from extended family members (parents, other relatives) or friends

- Lack of medical treatment ("My husband doesn't want me to see doctors")

- No access to checking accounts, cash, credit cards, etc. Having to ask for money

- Depression or anxiety and no counseling resources

- Decision-making done totally by spouse (financially, jobs, home, clothing, etc.)

- Fearful expressions if asked to be involved in an activity without spouse

- Total deference to spouse in all spiritual/religious beliefs

You might say, "If I experienced even *one* of those things, I'd be outta here!" Really? Consider this important statistic. A woman usually leaves five or six times before leaving permanently. Unfortunately, the anxiety level of the abuser has increased greatly by then; hence, the numbers of murders perpetrated by significant others remains high. Loss of the ability to control leads abusers into escalating actions over time.

Why does it take so long for women to leave? Because of fear, and because she made that promise: "For better or for worse." It gets cloudy when she tries to understand that the God we serve has already observed her partner breaking the wedding vows—those about honoring and protecting her, loving and serving her as He loves and serves His church. She often fails to see that the safety of her children, and at the very least, their training on how to have a loving relationship, is in jeopardy.

It is as if her reputation for keeping a promise at the altar becomes more important than the safety and salvation of her family! This comment comes with no unkindness. It's very hard to be in a compromised situation, leaving the victim unable to discern which way to go as opposing beliefs come at her from all directions.

Make no mistake. Divorce was never part of God's original plan. But that promise at the altar, rather than being another arbitrary rule to test our obedience quotient, is a statement of love and trust. Our God doesn't advocate divorce, but He also doesn't advocate anything that misrepresents His character. Because He won't be disobeyed? No! Rather, He knows what destroys, and He knows what heals. He desires for us to see Him as trustworthy, so we will work in unity with Him and allow Him to heal us. God never condones abuse!

THINK ABOUT IT

Doesn't it make sense to believe that what concerns God most is to see His children claim that He has given them the power and permission to abuse and destroy others? Do you believe God would want to have one of His beautiful daughters thinking they are somehow more spiritual because they allow themselves to be abused, believing they are actually honoring Him?

NOTES

DAY 5   How to Be a First Responder

Want to help those facing domestic violence? Here are some do's and don'ts of being that loving, understanding "first responder" to someone's pain:

1. Be a friend. Establish trust with someone who may be a victim so when they are ready, they will share with you.

2. Never discuss that person's problems with others without permission from the victim. Especially do not make them a subject of a Wednesday night prayer meeting in the name of holiness! ("Please pray for sister so-and-so, etc.") This is not just unkind; this could very well be a matter of life or death if the abuser hears about it.

3. Do encourage professional counseling but never suggest couple's counseling for domestic violence cases. The abuser will automatically shut down the victim, and may effectively pull the wool over the counselor's eyes.

4. Help from you should be in the form of discreet support, information about abuse, resource information (safe houses etc.), babysitting, and needed transportation.

5. Never try to force someone to leave a spouse. They have been forced and controlled long enough. It must be their decision. Respect that.

6. Do not try to reason with the abuser. This will only cause more abuse for the victim.

7. If safety is an issue and the victim is willing, don't hesitate to alert the police. Keep your own safety in mind. Loving others is not necessarily without risk.

8. Women should befriend women, and men should befriend men. Vital principle!

9. Don't let any codependent tendencies on your part involve you unhealthily. Do not "take it all on yourself." You are a first responder, not a fixer. We can only encourage, uplift, and support that victim.

10. Never go ahead of someone to their pastor or counselor. Trust would be broken.

THINK ABOUT IT

How do you understand *"obedience"*? Consider these quotes.

"Let the wife decide that it is the husband's prerogative to have full control of her body, and to mold her mind to suit his in every respect, and she yields her individuality; her identity is lost, merged in that of her husband. She is a mere machine for his will to move and control, a creature of his pleasure. He thinks for her, decides for her, and acts for her. She dishonors God in occupying this passive position" (*Testimonies on Sexual Behavior, Adultery, and Divorce*, E.G. White, p. 25).

"When the wife yields her body and mind to the control of her husband, being passive to his will in all things, sacrificing her conscience, her dignity, and even her identity, she loses the opportunity of exerting that mighty influence for good which she should possess, to elevate her husband" (Article by E. G. White in *Review and Herald*, Sept. 26, 1899).

"The spirit that Christ manifests toward us is the spirit that husband and wife are to manifest toward each other. Neither the husband nor the wife should attempt to exercise over the other an arbitrary control....You cannot do this and retain each other's love." (Article by E. G. White in *Review and Herald*, Dec. 10, 1908).

NOTES

DAY 6   What Church Leaders Can Do

If you are in a leadership position in a church, consider these actions, recommended by domestic violence researcher, René Drumm:

PREPARE yourself and members to effectively respond by: (1) Examining what the Bible has to say about violence and our responsibility to protect the vulnerable. (2) Becoming knowledgeable about the dynamics of abusive cycles. (3) Becoming familiar with abuse resources in your community and in the church, for both offenders and victims.

RESPOND by: (1) Taking every victim's accounts of abuse seriously. Don't say "I find that hard to believe." Instead, a good response is, "I'm so sorry you are going through this." (2) Place the responsibility for the abuse squarely on the abuser. (3) Reassure the victim that they do not deserve abuse. (4) Honor the decision of the victim to stay or leave. Safety is the primary consideration here.

ACT: (1) Condemn abuse of any type from the pulpit or from any position of leadership. (2) Be proactive by developing an abuse team as a support system for people in abusive situations. (3) Designate funds for abuse survivors.

THINK ABOUT IT

Doesn't it make perfect sense for churches to be the lighthouses—havens for hurting people? This two-edged sword may well be the reason we find broken, hurting folks right in our midst. Victims *and* perpetrators, (probably themselves victims in the past) need restoration. Abuse doesn't happen in a vacuum. There are always reasons why someone chooses to treat another with force.

We've identified the fact that fear plays a huge part in this. Fear also plays a part in the lack of first responders within the church. Fear of the unknown, however, can be liquidated. Facing these issues is not easy. But the reward of having helped someone through a really tough spot is incredible. Keep your ears and eyes open and your heart ready to serve, and God may well lay on your heart an opportunity for service. Moses thought he wasn't ready. Yet God was able to do great things through him. Be a Moses.

RESOURCES

If you're not comfortable with carrying resource cards, at least remember this: You can do an online search for "domestic violence resources in (*your city*)" and find help. Hopefully, your church will have brochures and/or business cards available in the women's bathrooms or in the vestibule with similar information.

On the Web, there are several training programs available. To locate resources, a list of domestic violence and abuse agencies worldwide can be found at: **www.hotpeachpages.net.** They can lead you to the nearest spouse abuse services.

NOTES

DAY 7   Our Real MO

DON'T STOP NOW!

Here are additional educational resources about domestic violence:

WEB:

faithtrustinstitute.org—Geared to victims and responders of all religions, with many training resources available, some in Spanish.

theraveproject.com—Religion and Violence E-learning's extensive website offers many resources for a caring Christian response to abuse.

gotquestions.org/domestic-violence.html—Biblical perspective into DV and specifically answers the question "What is the Christian response to DV?"

BOOKS:

The Battered Woman Syndrome, Lenore Walker

Understanding Violence Against Women, Nancy Crowell & Ann Burgess

The Abuse of Power: A Theological Problem, James Poling

TALK ABOUT IT

Abuse can happen anywhere—home, workplace, church, or government. Example: A newly hired manufacturing department head we will call Bill had mistakenly come to the conclusion that the company's owner was a tough, no-nonsense, do-it-my-way-or-it's-the-highway kind of person, and he chose to emulate that perceived character. From the get-go he put the hammer down on his own workers, raised production goal numbers, cut overtime, and loudly expressed his opinions. Bill wanted to be noticed! He was! The owner, whom he had never met, called Bill to his office.

Expecting to be promoted, he was definitely surprised to find that this family-oriented man who had built the business on trust, respect, employee participation, think tanks, company picnics, bonuses, and fairness was *not* who Bill had heard he was! It didn't take the owner long to acquaint Bill with his real modus operandi, and to kindly request that he run his department similarly. The owner knew that trust was at the top of his list, and that ultimately, working in unity cost the business much less than continual turnover and retraining. Thankfully, Bill was open to changing his opinion of the owner *and* his business paradigm.

Are we operating our lives based on information about our "owner" provided by the wrong source? What is *our* modus operandi?

AND FINALLY...

It works if you work it. That well-known recovery phrase is true. It falls short, however, if our endeavors are based on legalistic views of what we are *supposed* to do. Even being a first responder needs to happen from the heart.

NOTES

Domestic Violence in OUR Church?

WEEK 11

Tools of the Trade

DAY 1 Things Change After the Altar

LIVING WORDS

"Battered women are not constantly being abused....Understanding this cycle is very important if we are to learn how to stop or prevent battering incidents. This cycle also helps explain how battered women become victimized...and why they do not attempt to escape" (*The Battered Woman*, Lenore E. Walker, p. 55).

BOTTOM LINE

Take a close look at the cycle of abuse—the good, the bad, and the ugly.

SETTING THE STAGE

In the interest of fully understanding domestic violence, we will be spending some time this week looking at the cycle of battering or abuse. There are specific phases involved, and one of them tends to be the most confusing for the victims, often giving them false hope of better days to come.

Early on, there are still feelings of love, and the victims would give anything to see their lives become what they'd pictured—one of domestic peace. Children may be born as an attempt to glue the family unit together, thinking that the presence of little ones will soften the heart of the unstable partner. "Whatever you want, dear" is often spoken by the victim. Unfortunately, when any one person continually gives in to another's design for their spirit, they ultimately become a shadow person with no real passion for life.

Our design this week is for each of us to take a look at our own lives and be sure we are not living this shadowed existence. Take special heed, young single readers. Now is the time to learn the real meaning of "He *must* love me. Look how jealous he is!"

DAY 2 The Building Storm

Just like every cycle of life, abuse has its own repeating pattern. We find there are three distinct phases to the cycle, with no particular amount of time attached to each: (1) tension building (semi-quiet, walking on egg-shells phase), (2) explosion (acute battering incident), and (3) the calm, loving respite (honeymoon period – "I'm so sorry. It won't happen again!").

Sometimes a certain event may trigger the start of a next phase. Unfortunately, the cycle continues over and over. Like a hurricane, it seems to pick up strength as it goes, creating more and more havoc. And like a terrifying storm, there are periods of calm that fool the people involved into thinking it is over.

Ask any woman who has been through it year after year. She can tell you that it doesn't get better. What started out early in marriage as minor battles, disrespectful actions such as rolling of the eyes at a comment in public, walking out of a disagreement, or hiding a spouse's purse to prove a point, next time will be more acute, more purposeful, more acid. And through the years, the young man that wooed his beauty and promised to protect and provide becomes someone to be feared as he carries out his role as dictator instead of lover.

If the abuser has chosen "well," his dutiful wife will have gradually backed down and tried every passive behavior to calm his anger. Interestingly, most abusers are only that way in their own homes, knowing the general public will not be understanding. However, since society's laissez faire attitude passes right over her predicament for the most part, his secret is often very safe. With any previous home training at all, this once semi-gentle giant knows his behavior is inappropriate, but he knows no other way to control this woman whose increasingly distant aura seems to indicate he is losing her. He goes deeper into force and control, becomes oppressive, probably jealous, and develops an emotional tool box full of tricks, designed to keep his captive right where he wants her.

This same care-worn lady will go to the extreme, trying to control the environment so episodes of rage will not happen. When others speak of wondering about what is going on (maybe a close family member), the wife will literally make excuses for her spouse, cover up reality, and try to create the picture of marital bliss. In the process, she may actually alienate the very ones who could help her.

THINK ABOUT IT

If a victim is trying to get out of an abusive situation, which phase do you think would make it the most difficult? Does becoming passive help or hinder a solution? When she withdraws, what is the opposite reaction of the abuser? Could you recognize this cycle in a family unit very close to you?

NOTES

DAY 3   The Cycle - Phase One and Two

PHASE 1: TENSION BUILDING

There may be minor incidents during this time. The wife may believe she has done little things to irritate, and takes full responsibility. Her denial hides her anger at being treated this way.

Maybe he throws his dirty laundry at her, complaining that it is not already done. She is secretly happy that the episode wasn't worse, and she minimizes it and tries to forget it. Excuses like trouble at his work, the dog made a mess, or she was late for dinner cause her to believe it is of little consequence.

If the woman is a seasoned victim, she knows it will get worse. She still believes she can have some degree of control in keeping things from getting out of hand, but as tensions deepen, her ability to change things dissolves. He fears she will leave because he knows what he is doing is wrong, but that only heightens his fear and exacerbates his oppression of her.

Some couples have become adept at making this phase last for months or even years. But the inevitable is there, lurking nearby. The exhausted wife usually tries to withdraw or hide her feelings. He misinterprets everything, and finally the tension is unbearable.

PHASE 2: ACUTE INCIDENT

Something has to give. All the tension that has built up during phase one is let loose over some (unrelated, perhaps) incident. A need to control blinds the partner until he can't even understand his own actions, especially if alcohol or drugs are involved.

This will happen whether the woman has done anything irritating or not. It won't last as long as phase one or three; usually only a few hours. The victim may begin to talk of constant fatigue, headaches, hypertension, back pains, etc. Only the batterer can end this phase two. The woman's only option is to do something to stay safe. Whether she answers his verbal blasts or stays perfectly still, he will be enraged. In some instances, her cries will excite him even more.

Pain is not the biggest issue. Being psychologically trapped and unable to flee is her real concern. Some dissociate, knowing escape is futile. Afterwards, she may be thankful that it wasn't worse, believing that if he had been "his normal self" he wouldn't have said or done those things.

The tendency is to not seek medical help unless it is absolutely necessary. Depression and feelings of helplessness are common. It is easier to pretend it didn't happen if no one knows.

When she feels better, she may find the strength to call the police or go to a shelter. Records show that 80 percent of women usually call the police one to five times prior to being killed. Police hesitate to interrupt a phase-two battering incident with good reason. Usually the battering is worse after the police leave if they have tried to talk the couple down.

NOTES

DAY 4   The Cycle - Phase Three

PHASE 3: KINDNESS & CONTRITE, LOVING BEHAVIOR

Actually both parties are happy to see this phase begin. An absolute turnaround happens as the abuser begins to bathe the victim with extremely loving actions. There may be gifts, special dinners out. He realizes he has totally lost it, and wants to make amends. The tension has been released, and he becomes charming and loving. Forgiveness is asked for and given, and promises are made never to let it happen again. Oddly enough, this man may truly believe he will never do it again. Like an addict believing he's had his last drink, he cleanses his soul and is ready to walk on.

However, there is another part to it. He believes he has certainly taught her a lesson, and surely she will not ever do this "thing" that he can't stand. So of course, he won't have to retaliate again!

This is the phase where a woman can most likely get away. If she escaped hospitalization after a brutal attack, she will have been changed from a lonely, frightened little woman to being happy, and confident. Yes, she can *do* this—be independent, be safe!

But the batterer begins a new assault with flowers, candy, and cards. He may present himself to her close family members, begging them to intercede (which many do). What about the children, he reminds her. Then, if the couple attends church, the guilt feelings, "life commandments," and sermons begin to waft through their thoughts. Marriage is for life, they hear. God hates divorce. They may even worry about being a bad influence on others.

So, once again, the hope that it is over and that they will now be eternally happy rears its reassuring head. She becomes the "Queen of Denial," and chooses to remember the wonderful times in their early relationship. Those kind folks who are trying to help her get away may become disillusioned with her mind change, and distance themselves.

If she remains resolute and says she is leaving, the abuser's next technique may be to threaten suicide. Some carry it out. About ten percent of the men in one study killed themselves after the woman left. The reason is simple: If there is no one to control. What's left to live for?

Oh, what a tangled web we weave! Such a "symbiotic pair," so dependent that they literally believe they cannot exist without the other, no matter what happens.

Oddly, at some point in this trio of phases, the woman will lose even more respect for herself because she knows she sold her soul once again, willing to live through two awful phases in the future just to experience the "good one" for whatever time it may last—a brief moment, a few days, maybe longer.

THINK ABOUT IT

Am I a battered woman only if my husband beats me? Or if he just threatens to hurt me or takes away some privilege to teach me a lesson, is that battering, too?

NOTES

DAY 5   Rage Happens

Many women state that they were totally surprised with the first incident of battering. Further, there is no way to predict when it will happen again. There may be specific situations in which the woman fears retaliation due to extreme jealousy of others. And with that may come threats to harm those "others." A favorite pet may be hurt or even killed to signify what can be done to her if there is further reason for jealousy. Sometimes there are no recognizable warnings.

Severe psychological abuse usually precedes physical abuse. Some men are excellent name-callers, using a brainwashing technique where the woman always loses the battle. Guns or knives may enter the picture, with terror being the tool to degrade and dehumanize the spirit of the very woman they promised to protect.

The victim comes to believe that there is no way to change things, or to get away, believing that this spouse is practically omnipotent and can accomplish whatever he chooses with her. Yet, she also sees him as weak and fragile and she wants to help.   The Stockholm syndrome (a psychological phenomenon in which hostages express empathy and have positive feelings towards their captors, sometimes to the point of defending them) may play a part, some say.

It is almost impossible to imagine the damage done when rage is in control. Women in one study reported slaps, punches to the face and head, kicking, stomping, choking to the point of unconsciousness, pushing and shoving down stairs, severe shaking, arms twisted or broken, burns, scalding liquids, forced violent sexual acts, knife stabbings, and gunshot wounds. Broken ribs or limbs result from calculated punches or kicks by the man's hands and feet. Broken necks, backs, and limbs and even kidney injury and internal bleeding are reported along with eye injuries, broken noses, and teeth knocked out.

In *The Battered Woman*, Lenore E. Walker tells this story: "The first time Ira ever showed violence toward me was when his mother had come to visit us. We all went to see a movie together, and came back to our house. While I was fixing dinner for us, Ira and his mother were sitting at the table, and the three of us were talking about the movie we just saw. I didn't like what his mother said about one of the characters. I didn't agree with her, and I told her I thought she was wrong. Her interpretation of what had happened was different from mine. Ira became enraged. He threw the glass of water he was drinking at me. He then went to wipe me off, as I was dripping wet. As he was wiping me with a towel, he started slapping my face. His mother sat there without saying a word. I fled the room, absolutely shocked. It didn't happen again for another few months. And again, the next time was over a fight about his mother. Sometimes I think Ira really wasn't hitting me. He was really hitting his mother" (p. 86).

NOTES

DAY 6   Pornography and Money

Pornography: It bears repeating that pornography causes women to be seen simply as sex objects. Men, young and old, engaging in this addictive behavior, may cease to respect their girlfriends or spouses as they should. Brutality within the sexual relationship—if combined with an abusive personality—can be devastating. Some women literally stay with an abusive husband to keep from being single and thus exposing themselves to the chance of being raped by someone she doesn't know.

Money: Economics may also play a part. Perhaps we are tempted to believe that abuse happens only in the lower socioeconomic strata. If women were economically independent, they might not stay in an abusive marriage, we think. One of the tools used by a batterer is to keep his wife out of the professional circuit or at least to lock away earnings so there is no access to them. Somehow women—even those who have inherited money—seem to feel that the man of the house controls it.

Here is Christina's story from *The Battered Woman:*

"I finally decided to leave him. I had had enough. Even though he became extraordinarily violent only once or twice a year, the psychological harassment and minor incidents became too much to bear. Though I was fearing another incident which I felt impending, I filed divorce papers. Within a short time, the Internal Revenue Service filed a claim with my attorney charging me $35,000 in taxes that represented my share of the income Russell was earning. Although I never saw most of that money, as far as the government was concerned, this is what I owed them. On my $18,000 salary per year, I simply couldn't afford it. So Russell and I decided to try to live together again. What a mistake. Before the year was out, I had almost killed him in defending myself from another brutal beating. Fortunately, a court hearing determined that my fair share of the back taxes was a much more reasonable sum of money" (p. 28).

In that toolbox marked "fear" we find one of the best ways to trap a woman in a relationship: through her fear of becoming poor. Or, in the reverse, money might be used as a coercive lasso, no matter the socioeconomic status. Fear that the man might quit working and claim that he has nothing to give her in a separation or divorce is often well founded.

Whether she stays or goes, money may well be used as a weapon. He may get angry if she doesn't have enough money left from his check to pay the bills. He may pay all the bills and leave her nothing for groceries or even a small clothing allowance. Another dream dashed.

NOTES

DAY 7   Getting Help

DON'T STOP NOW!

Obviously, we've looked at some pretty heavy things this week. Rather than doing more research, it might be good to do something nice for yourself. Take a mini-vacation, maybe a picnic by the river, or visit a good friend. Engulf yourself with the good stuff of life, and count your blessings.

If you need to get professional help because you are personally in an abusive situation, make that call and begin the process. That is the best gift you could give yourself. Remember that there is never an excuse for abuse. God does not condone it, but He loves the victim and the perpetrator. Both are His children, but He wants to protect one from the other if necessary, just as you would if they were your children, abusing one another. Find joy in remembering you are His child.

TALK ABOUT IT

Set aside a couple of hours in a quiet place. Take a tablet of paper and write your own story. Write about how you grew up, about your relationship with your parents, teachers, pastors, employers, spouses. Don't skip the painful parts or the very happy parts. This may take a while, but it will be of inestimable value.

Then, rewrite your life. Write what you *wish* it had been like. Write about how you wish your parents and others had treated you. If the stories match, great. If not, ask yourself if you have been able to heal from the hurts. See whether you can go back through your original story and identify the ways in which your (or your parents') image of God may have colored the events. Try rewriting those events using a healthier paradigm of God and His universal law of love. Then rejoice that you have learned some incredible things about our Heavenly Father so that as you pass "life" on to others, you can change history. It is never too late.

AND FINALLY...

We certainly have not exhausted the information on abuse. But are you beginning to get a clearer picture? There is someone out there you may be able to touch that no one else can. Be open to that.

NOTES

Domestic Violence in OUR Church?

WEEK 12

My Role

DAY 1   No Man Is an Island

LIVING WORDS

A woman who had lost her baby asked a holy man if there was a cure for her grief. "Yes," he replied. "You must find a house that has never known sorrow. Take a mustard seed from that house, and you will be cured." She never found any such house.

BOTTOM LINE

No man is an island. We're interconnected in ways we may not even recognize.

SETTING THE STAGE

We're nearing the end of our study on domestic violence. Much of it has been rather heavy information to assimilate and hopefully some soul searching has occurred. Now we want to look at what to do with this information. We definitely don't want to be "more informed prisoners," agitated by our newfound education but scared to apply it.

Perhaps we are like a young graduate having been hired for a new job and wondering how he will fulfill the requirements. Maybe we have had our eyes opened to situations around us, and are determined to allow God's love to filter through us as we become the "lighthouse" for those in need. We may have even realized that we are reflected in some of the stories and information and need dissolution.

Are you gathering strength to set boundaries or make huge changes for safety sake? Is there someone you need to befriend? Whichever the case and however anxious we may be, there is the assurance that our Heavenly Father walks with us in this abusive world, having experienced what we have experienced and desiring that we recognize His incredible ability to uplift, resolve, and keep safe those in need.

DAY 2 What Is My Role?

Be assured that not everyone is called to be a first responder. You will know if God has asked you to do it. However, there's usually no ray of self-assurance that accompanies His request, so don't wait until you feel qualified.

Earlier, we mentioned Moses. He needed a partner and God allowed Aaron to go with him. There may well be a partner for you. Or you may become a part of a group that desires to help lift burdens.

"But there are many more ways to reach people for Christ," you may say. Yes, there are. But what higher calling is there? Listen to these words found in Matthew 25:34-40: "Then the King will say to those on his right, 'Come, you who are blessed by my Father, inherit the kingdom prepared for you from the foundation of the world. For I was hungry and you gave me food, I was thirsty and you gave me drink, I was a stranger and you welcomes me, I was naked and you clothed me, I was sick and you visited me, I was in prison and you came to me.... Truly, I say to you, as you did it to one of the least of my brothers, you did it to me."

Christ thought it important enough to mention that those who have done this, have done it unto *Him*, and will be with Him throughout eternity.

Once again, we must apply the principle of freedom to choose. Only by love is love awakened. Only as we love others more than self (not *instead* of self), can we truly serve in the way God designed. Only when we can hand our fears to God who never uses inappropriate power over us, can He relieve the anxiety that keeps us tied to self-preservation. When we realize, as did Brennan Manning, that there are really no "others" but we are all one, can we find ourselves serving from the heart— not from fear of requirements and legalities, but through loving service.

When Mary anointed the feet of Jesus, she knew she'd be judged by Simon and his guests. She may not have been sure what Jesus Himself would think. But her heart overflowed with love for what He had done for her. Many believe that she's the same Mary who had been caught in adultery. Whoever she was, she obviously had much for which to thank Him. Do you? Can there ever be enough perfume available to honor our Savior? Will we, even through eternity, be able to share all of our feelings of gratitude with Him?

Don't worry. God knows how you feel. Getting to know you personally is what He, His Son, and the Holy Spirit set out to accomplish through Christ's life here on earth. When at last we share His throne, they will be satisfied.

NOTES

DAY 3   Tears in Heaven

In our sanctified imagination, let's think a bit more about heaven and how it might be for our Savior, not just for us. To finally have His children home, to know no one will ever again abuse another, to feel the thanksgiving and praise we will offer, and to see us healthy and happy: *that* will be His joy.

When a soldier comes home from war whole, his thankful family certainly rejoices. When we go home to heaven, what rejoicing there will be!   We will no doubt be able to sit at Jesus' feet and learn through eternity how He protected and guided us. We will see that along with allowing us freedom of choice, the Holy Spirit guided us into all truth and gave us the strength to share it with others.

There must be a special place for those who have suffered much on earth—perhaps for their beliefs, but also perhaps they were in a relationship that wasn't what God planned. Those dear ones will fully realize for the first time that God did not cause their pain nor did he condone the actions that caused it. We're told there will be no tears in heaven. I believe that may be a figurative statement. From my human perspective, I can't possibly imagine a dry eye in the congregation as these domestic abuse stories are reviewed and we see the divine guidance that was received.

Surely our guardian angels will be thrilled to finally talk with us face to face and tell us what they have done, with God's direction, in our lives. What incredible lessons we will learn about who God really is and how He used His sovereign power without ever once using inappropriate force.

Justice by the world's standard means punishment—vindictive measures, an eye for an eye. But *heavenly* justice might look like this: The perpetrator—forgiven, healed, and renewed, joining in the chorus. The murderer—won over by God's unconditional love, perhaps sent to the electric chair by the state, but saved by God's grace because he finally "got it." And yes, the thief on the cross— present and accounted for.

We rejoice when one gives his or her heart to Christ. Can you imagine the joy of the heavenly host combining with the happiness of that multitude of saints who, down through the ages, have been changed into God's image because they recognized Satan's lies and decided that God could be trusted after all? *That* is justice.

DAY 4   Knowing God

In Ty Gibson's book, *An Endless Falling in Love*, he describes a courtship that took place by email with no pictures sent. The two began to realize they were in love and yet, despite the young man's pleas, his cyber friend refused to send a picture. She wanted him to learn to love her for who she was, not what she looked like.

There was a happy ending, just so you know. But it reminds us of our love relationship with God, as Gibson says. No one has actually seen Him. He has given us love letters, flowers, gifts galore, and the beauty of the world to show us His love. Still, we have not seen the actual person of God.

Some have, but very few knew it. The song "Mary Did You Know?" often brings tears to listeners' eyes. The lyrics ask Mary if she knew that when she kissed the face of baby Jesus, she was kissing the face of God!

In this day and time, we must be satisfied with writings and hearsay. We must have "faith" that He exists. Some say faith is blind. Some say love is blind. However, in the appropriate context, neither statement is true. Can you truly love someone or have faith in them until you have come to *trust* them—to know who they are? Blind faith has gotten many into trouble. Getting into an abusive relationship is a good example of blind faith. Anyone who has trusted a financial advisor only to lose hundreds or even millions of dollars might recognize the foolishness of blind faith.

God has never asked us to love Him without evidence. He's never asked us to love Him blindly. In His openness and love, He has told us story after story of how He treats even His enemies. Through life experiences, He constantly reminds us of His loving care. And as we spend time communing with Him, we receive strength and assurance of His presence. The unity, the oneness (at-one-ment—atonement) fulfills our deepest needs and allows us to receive His grace and spirit daily.

Forgiveness? *His* was put in place from the foundation of the worlds! Today we can recognize it, let it break our hearts, and guide us to trust a God who would do such a thing.

As we come to know the type of relationship God wants to have with us, as we see the truth about a God who never abuses, never belittles, never misguides, and as we soak in those truths, only then can we become children, lovers, parents, grandparents who can be trusted—who would rather die than harm another human being.

THINK ABOUT IT

How can we understand the mind of Christ? Does the Rx of "Bible study, prayer, and share" guarantee a relationship with Christ, or can it only be accomplished through a full understanding of who He is? What could keep us from understanding God?

NOTES

DAY 5 How Can I Let You Go?

"For I know the plans I have for you, declares the Lord, plans for welfare and not for evil, to give you a future and a hope"(Jeremiah 29:11).

How *do* we get acquainted with God? "There is no clearer picture of God than may be seen at the foot of the cross. God had told the truth when he warned that the wages of sin is death. In his Son he was dying that death. But God was not executing his Son. He only 'gave him up,' as he will give up the wicked at the end. And though by rights we should have died, God did not ask us to prove the truthfulness of His word. He sacrificed himself in his Son. What more could God do to warn us of our sin and win us back to faith? Surely he had shown himself infinitely worthy of our trust" (*Can God Be Trusted?*, Graham Maxwell, p. 82).

If you believe there is life on other planets, have you ever thought what the inhabitants think of God? As soon as sin flickered into a flame, Satan made sure that God's character was called into question. It was at the cross that God's righteousness was expressed most clearly. It is only here on earth that any doubt about who God is still exists. The universe saw that He was who He said He was, and that He was love, willing to sacrifice Himself to save us.

Some believe that God will be angry at the wicked as they die in the last day. But those are His children who have chosen not to accept His love. God does not change. His love for them remains. Just as Christ cried over Jerusalem, our Heavenly Father will be heard to say, "How can I give you up? How can I let you go?" Thousands of years and the resources of heaven have been spent to prove His love. Far beyond the grief an earthly father feels at the loss of his son, is the grief God will feel at losing those children who refuse to accept His gift. This gift was planned by Father and Son together—the ultimate sacrifice experienced by both.

Satan has tried to convince us that Jesus stands between us and an angry God, begging God not to spill our blood. What kind of a god would require blood to forgive? Heathen perhaps? We picture a God who rages in anger against His Son's earthly friends, and in an effort to save them, Jesus convinces His Father to kill Him instead! How can we attribute such brutality to this loving Father? I think sometimes God weeps.

THINK ABOUT IT

If you were Satan and wanted to win over as many people as possible, wouldn't the cross and its true purpose be the very light you'd want to darken? Wouldn't the relationship between Father and Son be next? And God's character? Change that and you've got everyone—not just Christians.

NOTES

DAY 6   Perfect Love

It's no stretch of the imagination to understand how so-called "religious" beliefs can obliterate the image of the true God in our minds and hearts. The *really* Good News is that God is *not* the kind of person Satan has made Him out to be. He does not ask us to serve Him through fear.

"There is no fear in love, but perfect love casts out fear. For fear has to do with punishment, and whoever fears has not been perfected in love. We love because he first loved us. If anyone says, 'I love God,' and hates his brother, he is a liar; for he who does not love his brother whom he has seen cannot love God whom he has not seen" (1 John 4:18-20).

When the children of Israel stood at the foot of Mount Sinai, Moses assured them that they had no need to be afraid of God. Today, although God sometimes speaks with a loud voice to get our attention, He seems to prefer His "still, small voice." Maybe that is why we think He is silent when we *want* Him to speak directly to us.

One thing is certain: the most awesome yet terrible words He will ever utter are those spoken when all of man's final decisions have been made. "If you are determined to walk away from me, I have to let you go!" He says in love.

Sin kills. Finally, this old earth will be cleansed with fire. Then God will place here, once again, the original Eden for us to enjoy for eternity.

THINK ABOUT IT

Will it be safe to allow you entrance into heaven? Do you quote scripture but speak and mutter against your brother...or wife...or husband? Or do you long for the day when all will be of one spirit? Do you long to hear those words: "Welcome home, children"?

Love knows no limit to its patience. God is waiting for us to make our decision so we can live where His beautiful law of liberty extends freedom and joy to all. No more anger, no more abuse, no more sadness. What a day that will be!

DAY 7   Soaking Up Truth

DON'T STOP NOW!

Suggested Reading:

Can God Be Trusted? by Graham Maxwell

Myth of a Christian Nation by Gregory Boyd

Could It Be This Simple? by Timothy Jennings

The Ultimate Prescription by James L. Marcum

An Endless Falling in Love by Ty Gibson

Study prayerfully each resource you find in your hands, asking God to lead in your understanding. Everyone has the freedom to decide how they see God, and how they let it affect their life.

It is the prayer of the author of these lessons that God's character of love will shine through and that truth will fill our hearts, changing us more and more into the image of God. When He comes, may He find a group of people—many people—looking for and recognizing Him because they have come to truly *know* who He is.

TALK ABOUT IT

She sat in a straight chair after inviting me to make myself comfortable on her sofa. I informed her how the interview would go, and turned on the recorder. This woman who had been married to a physician, now lived in an aged, redecorated frame cottage. Her story went something like this:

"In the beginning, we were very happy. I was glad to finally be married to someone who seemed so strong in the church. I became his office manager. We had a lovely home. Gradually his attitude toward me changed. I could do nothing right. I sensed another relationship going on in the office. Our times alone practically ceased, and although he continued to look good and smell good at church and at work, at home he was scary.

"I became his whipping post, if not physically, at least emotionally or verbally. Then, when he hit me, I decided that was it. Even though I walked away with practically nothing, I am so much happier. It has been hard to continue in the church, but I know that just because he does not reflect Christ, it doesn't mean that the church is at fault.

"The pastor wouldn't talk to me, but I have to believe he also is an exception to the rule. I hope this will help you in your research, because I know I am one of many. I have met some of them."

AND FINALLY...

That partial interview is only one of many conducted by members of the Christian Abuse Response Education (CARE) team at Southern Adventist University. Most victims expressed a great need to be listened to, and believed. Are you a good listener?

NOTES

Domestic Violence in OUR Church?

WEEK 13

Hope for the Future

DAY 1   The Human Struggle

LIVING WORDS

"Failure to recognize the value of merely being with God, as the beloved, without doing anything, is to gouge the heart out of Christianity" (*Abba's Child*, Brennan Manning). Someone who has grown close to the true God, and who has been changed by Him, *will not abuse.*

BOTTOM LINE

Man cannot serve two masters. Period.

SETTING THE STAGE

People can appear to serve both good and evil. Living two lives is not new to our generation. One only has to watch a bit of reality TV to see that the hidden secrets of people's lives create quite a dichotomy as they perform in separate ways, in separate realms. The "old man" and the "new man" live in each of us. Like the Apostle Paul, we do what we don't want to do, and we don't do what we want to do. The human struggle will continue until Christ makes the world new.

In this final lesson, we will pull together the goals, tools, and outcomes of abuse. We will be reminded that Christ's tools are diametrically opposed to Satan's. We will discuss what the church *is* doing to help, and where they fall short. Remember, we are part of that church.

NOTES

DAY 2 Reviewing the Lessons

Lesson 1: God's design for the intimate relationship has been pictured as the ultimate avenue for understanding who God is and the love He offers. We see that God needs functional families to draw the world to Himself.

Lesson 2: Satan's plan to destroy the home and his evil connivings have been unveiled. We have begun to sift through his toolbox, one he bequeaths to men and women in many households. We have seen the damage done to mankind through the damage done to God's image.

Lesson 3: Customs for women and for men have been reviewed—in the home, in the church, and in society. The effect of such customs on relationships in and out of the home has been exposed.

Lesson 4: We've stated the definition of abuse: Any act intended to instill fear and exert control over another person. Remember, we all do random acts that may be somewhat abusive for which we are sorry. It is the continual, escalating habit of using tools *designed to control* that explains the abuser.

Lesson 5: We have examined man's role as husband and father with far-reaching consequences, and had our eyes opened to both functionality and dysfunction.

Lesson 6: Abuse is passed down to the generations that follow. Researching this issue has helped us understand how we may generate some hope of staunching the flow.

Lesson 7: We've used God's Word to explain both abuse and the opposite—unconditional love. It has shown us how men and women *should* treat each other.

Lesson 8: Children's roles and how they learn to be abusers demonstrated the life-changing effects that abuse has on them.

Lesson 9: Importantly, we then took a look at whether God abuses *His* power. We've seen that our view of God can greatly color how we treat others. This may be the most important lesson of the thirteen.

Lesson 10: There are helpful tips on what we as church family members should and should not say to those in need. There are resources. Privacy and freedom are addressed.

Lesson 11: The cycle of violence—what it actually looks like in a home, and what tools are used along the way—was our next lesson.

Lesson 12: We learned about what our role can be. We were reminded that we are first responders, not fixers.

THINK ABOUT IT

This is the time to review any of these topics where you feel you do not have a good foundation. If you are in a class, ask questions. If the lessons are too brief to give you all the information you need, go to the resource materials. Don't let this be the end of your studies.

NOTES

DAY 3   Seeing Saul/Paul

It would be unfortunate to complete this series without mentioning one of the most exciting transformations of an abuser recorded in history: Saul of Tarsus.

In Acts 22, Paul tells his own story. Saul (his name before God reached down and spoke to him audibly) believed he was doing God's will. There are men today who are sincerely trying to lead their family in the way they think God dictates. Saul was sincerely *wrong*. And because of his messed-up image of God, he persecuted (abused) many Christians.

This is one time God couldn't use His still, small voice. Saul wasn't listening! But the bright light incident on the way to Damascus got his attention. Sometimes it takes something larger than life to get the attention of an abuser. But there was hope for this perpetrator, and what glorious "justice" was done! God healed Saul the perpetrator, and pronounced him Paul the protector of the very ones he had been hurting, making him the carrier of the truly Good News.

Sometimes, with the abuser's true repentance and permission, God can work miracles in their life. And what better person to help others than someone healed of that disease! The hard part of that scenario is that the victim really can't afford to take the *abuser's* word that he is healed. There must be evidence over time. Often that means separation while both parties heal. Paul certainly had to take time to show the church that he would no longer persecute them before they could trust him.

One important point to remember is that forgiving someone does *not* equal trusting them. Jesus forgave the ones who put Him on the cross. That did not mean they were trustworthy, or saved. Many victims of abuse or crime believe that if they forgive, that means they must let that person back into their lives. Not necessarily. Forgiveness and trust are two separate and distinct things. Forgiveness comes from the heart of a victim, and from God. It may also, in time, come from the heart of the perpetrator towards himself/herself. But trust takes time to rebuild.

Paul has many good things to teach us in God's Word, but perhaps this lesson applies best to our studies this quarter. We can thank him for recording his experience and showing what God is willing to do for even the vilest offender.

At times, we humans have to get out of the way and let God do His work.

NOTES

DAY 4   Elder Abuse

It is fitting that, at the end of our studies, we at least lightly address the ending years of life—that feared "last hurrah!"

In the book *Ripe* by Janet Champ and Charlotte Moore, the writers suggest a positive approach: "What if this great endless valley before us is really more of an undiscovered paradise? A garden where once again we—aren't we lucky?—get to pick fruit from the Tree of Knowledge instead of the Tree of Benign Ignorance? It could be, it may be, that what we're headed for isn't the dark ages at all but something altogether lighter. Brighter. Be. Not. Afraid. Things may get a little messy. You may get a little messy. But that's the way it is meant to be. Life itself is messy and ripe, waiting to be picked rough skin and all. After all, it's not the end of the world. It's not even the end of your own private cul-de-sac. It's the next chapter. The next beginning. It's the rest of your life. And lucky you: You get to live it" (p. 23).

At the receipt of that first AARP bulletin, we feel the gut twinge and a bit of animosity toward anyone who suggests we are "old." Each decade or so brings new fears, especially at that point of no return called "full retirement." "What now?" we ask. "Who am I now that I'm not a (*fill in your profession*)? Do I even matter? Am I a nuisance to children, friends, society? Can I find the energy to be a positively remembered grandparent? What *happened* while I was sleeping? I used to be able to remember five minutes ago. I used to turn cartwheels in the grass, ski barefoot, ride horses across a grassy field, and speak with authority. I must have blinked!"

Youth, as well as health and independence, are ultimate losses. Children may become our parents, directing our lives or allowing an institution to do so. Doctors prescribe "amount and frequency" and we obey. Self becomes blurred.

Elder abuse, we like to think, is rare. But reports are increasing. Caretakers, who know their turn is coming, lose patience. Anger spills out for whatever reason. Who is there to protect the elderly?

Perhaps the best advice to be given here is to *listen*. Don't discount what you hear from older friends and family members as simply paranoia. Maintain due diligence just to be sure.

If you are still young, find a way to glean all the knowledge that remains resident in the minds of maturing senior citizens. Their life stories are, many times, incredible. Make it your study to discover why some elders are so delightful, and others impossible. Use that information to help you on your own journey.

Learn to stay healthy so the latter years can be enjoyed, not endured. And find in your heart a place for your "elder neighbor" who needs you. Grandmas and grandpas, even if they aren't your real ones, have much love to give.

NOTES

DAY 5   This Was Foretold

Whether it's called domestic violence, intimate partner violence, spouse abuse, child abuse, or elder abuse, we have hopefully begun to see it as it really is—the effort to control another person. We have traced the pattern of an abuser as he/she deceptively weaves a web of control, while destroying self-assurance, personality, and passion. Whether it is ever registered in a police precinct file or not, it is still a crime.

Reducing another to a slave physically or mentally or taking the spirit and hope from another can be as devastating as discovering one has a terminal illness. The victim may indeed wish for an illness, just so they can simply fade away.

If depression becomes deep enough, suicide is often considered. Or, in self defense after years of abuse, a spouse may finally explode and murder their abuser.

"In the last days there will come times of difficulty. For people will be lovers of self, ... arrogant, abusive, ... ungrateful, ... heartless, ... without self-control, brutal, not loving good, treacherous, reckless, ... having the appearance of godliness, but denying its power" (2 Timothy 3:1-5).

When interpreted correctly, there is *nothing* in the Bible that condones abuse. Rightly understood, the admonition that man is to be the "head" of the woman, means he is her protector, to love her like Christ loves the church.

Researchers estimate that as many as twenty percent of couples in the United States experience intimate partner violence. Nearly 4.5 million incidents of violence toward women and 2.9 million incidents toward men occur in the U.S. yearly. In 2000, the FBI reported that thirty-two percent of all female murder victims were killed by their current or former spouses or boyfriends; three percent of male murder victims were killed by their current or former spouses or girlfriends.

Intimate partner violence homicide victims are seventy-six percent female and twenty-four percent male. Nonfatal violent crimes by intimate partners account for twenty percent among women, and three percent for males. Interestingly, sixty percent of murders by young people, ages 15 to 21, are the killing of their mother's abuser.

Research in the Seventh-day Adventist Church (1,431 church-affiliated responders) suggested other areas of abuse. Forty-four percent said they had experienced being told what to do with expected obedience; forty percent had been insulted, sworn at, or called names. Thirty-three percent were ignored or had their accomplishments discounted. Twenty-nine percent said spouses made big family decisions without asking them (job changes, financial, vacation, education, etc.). Twenty-eight percent noted being limited in involvement with friends, family, coworkers.

No church is exempt. People are people. But maybe we have been able to identify the baseline reason for abuse: *How we see God*. If we see Him as abusive, vindictive, vengeful, and we are supposed to be "like" Him, *we* may abuse. Isn't it high time that we as God's people—carrying His name "Christian"—discover the reason for abusive behavior and do something about it, not by force, but by loving service to others and by accepting forgiveness and grace ourselves?

NOTES

DAY 6   Things Are Opening Up

Christianity has seen with closed eyes and heard with stopped up ears, the reality that abuse exists within the church, both in leadership and in families. Thankfully, that is gradually changing. Churches are beginning to recognize dysfunction within their ranks and are addressing it.

Sadly, we are not the head but the tail in this endeavor. TV personalities, books, and magazines are way ahead of us. But there's hope. Pastors are beginning to preach sermons concerning domestic violence. Support groups are appearing. Guest speakers and trainers are being invited to the sanctuaries. Headway is being made.

Slowly, the historical lack of awareness, education, pastoral skills, resources, as well as blaming the victim and believing the abuser, is gradually morphing into positive solutions and hope for the abused. First responder pastors are becoming more numerous.

Wouldn't it be nice to redo the survey in a few years and find that women are beginning to say, "My pastor was so helpful! He made me feel I was believed. And when the facts bore me out, he was helpful in finding me a place to go." Maybe that woman would say "My friend Mary at church was aware enough to seek me out and get me to talk. From that talk, I sought help and now I and my children are safe."

NOTES

DAY 7   Choose This Day

DON'T STOP NOW!

What can you do in your own church?

- Ask your pastor to address the issue from the pulpit. If he has not attended any training programs, encourage him to do so. Share with him how to take this course.

- Advocate for a first responder group who can plan for materials, funds, and resources for those who need them.

- Become a good listener and someone who is known as a loyal friend in time of need.

- Remember, safety is the first issue. Stress this to victims, to your response committee, and be safe yourself.

- Always be discreet with information entrusted to you, respecting privacy and promoting safety.

TALK ABOUT IT

Dr. David McClelland of Harvard University studied 132 Harvard students, and showed that the immune system is strengthened by forty-one percent immediately after watching a video of Mother Teresa helping people in Calcutta. Six hours later they were still stronger. What we see (TV / computer / life) can either strengthen or destroy our immune systems.

What do you think happens in the body during abuse? When the body is attacked with negative emotions, the body lowers its guard and provides an open door for disease. People's hearts are failing them for fear. Heart disease claims 1,000 victims per day.

There are many ways to murder someone else or yourself, even slowly and imperceptibly. According to the World Health Organization, depression is the second leading cause of death in women under the age of 44, and will soon be the second leading cause of death in all people in the modern world. The term "para-suicide" means allowing a subtle and protracted pattern of behavior to result in premature death. It means not taking proper care of yourself or your spouse in order to produce this phenomenon.

Honor and revere life at every level. A human being is a powerful thing. We have been given power to create or destroy. Don't misuse it.

This information is not meant to awaken in us the feeling that we are responsible for the salvation of everyone on the planet. Rather, it reminds us how great a privilege we have in being part of God's incredible plan for health and happiness. It begins at home.

AND FINALLY...

Choose ye this day whom you will serve. Will it be the type of god who is cruel, vengeful, and angry? Or will you turn to the One True God, the lover of our souls? Creator, Healer, Savior. The choice, and the privilege, is ours.

NOTES

ABOUT US

Come and Reason Ministries is dedicated to helping you learn to discern, to stimulate you to think, to help hone and refine your reasoning powers, and to increase your ability to know right from wrong and healthy from unhealthy. We're not here to tell you what to think, but to show you how to more efficiently use your God-given reasoning power to better grow in grace and experience a closer walk with God.

DISCOVER MORE

Want to learn more about Come and Reason Ministries? Visit us online today and get life-transforming information on Bible principles for better mental health, Christian growth, healthier families and relationships, strengthening the mind and body, human sexuality, and so much more!

Blogs on Current Topics • Podcasts • Seminars • Bible Study Guides
Answers to Difficult Bible Questions • Weekly Bible Study Class

All this and more–FREE!
comeandreason.com

Also find us on:

More Books from Come and Reason & Dr. Timothy Jennings

THE AGING BRAIN

The choices you make today can help you maintain your vitality, mind, and independence as you get older. Filled with simple, practical steps, *The Aging Brain* is an easy-to-use guide to maintaining brain and body health throughout your life and avoiding the diseases and problems people face as we age.

THE GOD-SHAPED HEART

Exposes a single idea, misunderstood and deeply rooted within Christianity, that has prevented millions from experiencing the freedom and healing of God's unfailing love.

THE GOD-SHAPED BRAIN

A compelling, evidence-based case for a God of love and His methods that is easy to understand, revealing why it is so important to live in harmony with God and His design for life.

COULD IT BE THIS SIMPLE?

Describes in simple language how your mind is designed by God to work and what happens when it goes awry. Provides straightforward methods for reestablishing your mind in a healthy balance.

A NEW PARADIGM

A fascinating new look at God's healing plan as taught in Jewish sanctuary symbolism that will transform your picture of God and change your heart forever!

THE REMEDY

An enhanced, modern English paraphrase of the New Testament that will breathe new life into your Bible study experience.

Find these resources at comeandreason.com or at amazon.com.